THE
ELISSAS

THE ELISSAS

Three Girls, One Fate, and the Deadly Secrets of Suburbia

SAMANTHA LEACH

LEGACY
LIT

NEW YORK   BOSTON

Copyright © 2023 by Samantha Leach

Cover design by Dana Li. Cover image by Getty Images. Cover copyright © 2023 by Hachette Book Group, Inc.

Legacy Lit
Hachette Book Group
1290 Avenue of the Americas
New York, NY 10104
LegacyLitBooks.com
Twitter.com/LegacyLitBooks
Instagram.com/LegacyLitBooks

First Edition: June 2023

Legacy Lit is an imprint of Grand Central Publishing. The Legacy Lit name and logo are trademarks of Hachette Book Group, Inc.

The publisher is not responsible for websites (or their content) that are not owned by the publisher.

The Hachette Speakers Bureau provides a wide range of authors for speaking events. To find out more, go to hachettespeakersbureau.com or email HachetteSpeakers@hbgusa.com.

Legacy Lit books may be purchased in bulk for business, educational, or promotional use. For information, please contact your local bookseller or the Hachette Book Group Special Markets Department at special.markets@hbgusa.com.

Library of Congress Cataloging-in-Publication Data
Names: Leach, Samantha, author.
Title: The Elissas : three girls, one fate, and the deadly secrets of suburbia / Samantha Leach.
Description: First edition. | New York, NY : Legacy Lit, [2023]
Identifiers: LCCN 2022057941 | ISBN 9780306826917 (hardcover) | ISBN 9780306826931 (ebook)
Subjects: LCSH: Teenage girls—Institutional care. | Youth—Services for. | Opioid abuse.
Classification: LCC HQ798 .L42 2023 | DDC 362.73/2—dc23/eng/20230123
LC record available at https://lccn.loc.gov/2022057941

ISBNs: 9780306826917 (hardcover), 9780306826931 (ebook)

Printed in the United States of America

LSC-C

Printing 1, 2023

For DD, who always believed I could

Hell is a teenage girl.

—*JENNIFER'S BODY*, 2009

Author's Note

January 23, 2023

Though I first started trying to tell some version of this story back in 2011—in the creative writing workshops I took in the wake of Elissa's death, eager to transmute the details of our friendship onto the page—the process of compiling this book began in earnest in the fall of 2019. Just months after Alyssa passed away, and nearly three years after Alissa had died as well.

In the almost four years that I've worked on *The Elissas*, I've spoken to over sixty people and reached out to countless more. While I went to great lengths to interview nearly every living person mentioned in the book, there were some subjects who were unreachable or simply uninterested in talking with me. In cases where those subjects featured more prominently in the story, I changed their identifying characteristics for purposes of anonymity. Those subjects—along with all others featured in the book, excluding myself and the Elissas—were also given pseudonyms.

It was through these conversations that I crafted both the scenes and the dialogue that you find in this book. Without the Elissas here to speak for themselves, I relied on the recollections of those closest to them to capture the spirit of the stories depicted in the following pages. These stories have also been fleshed out through my exhaustive reporting on these women, as I've incorporated my perspective on what they would be thinking, feeling, and experiencing in any given moment.

Throughout my reporting, I also made great efforts to speak with representatives for each of the programs that were mentioned at length. Only some of those administrators chose to reply, and their responses have been included where they either contradict or clarify details shared by other interview subjects. Ultimately, the aim of *The Elissas* is not to issue a blanket indictment of the Troubled Teen Industry, nor should any mention of a program in the book be taken as an indictment or accusation. Rather, this is my endeavor to honor the lives of Elissa, Alissa, and Alyssa, which were taken far too soon.

THE
ELISSAS

I'd been dreading going to Nebraska for most of the summer. My trip was set for mid-August, just two months before the ten-year anniversary of Elissa's death. In the first few years after she died, any tether to Elissa on the calendar—her birthday, the day she died at just eighteen years old, the date of her funeral— would derail me. But as more time passed, I started feeling like they no longer warranted a breakdown. Now I was twenty-eight, living in New York City, and working in journalism. The life that I'd been manifesting ever since Elissa and I were children had materialized. And while I felt a profound pull to go to Nebraska, to visit Ponca Pines Academy, the place where Elissa spent her last school days, my fear over what the experience might elicit was even more potent. It could unleash the deeply buried grief that still gnawed at me. Unresolved and uncomfortable.

Elissa and I were infants when we met, going on to attend nursery, elementary school, and temple together. Elissa wasn't just my first friend; she was my favorite friend. She was boisterous, unabashed, brazen. In first grade, I sheepishly showed her the wart on my finger I'd been hiding underneath a Band-Aid, only to have her rip her shoe off and expose the ones that lined the bottoms of her feet. When my breasts blossomed before hers in fifth grade, she wore a bra alongside me in solidarity. By seventh grade we'd started partying together, stealing coconut rum from the bar at my grandmother's house and taking swigs before logging on to AIM, tipsily IMing our friends and crushes. We shared these early acts of rebellion before our paths diverged, before Elissa was sent away to Ponca Pines, and I stayed behind, forced to forge my own identity within our hometown.

Ponca Pines wasn't a traditional high school. It was a therapeutic boarding school and part of the Troubled Teen Industry: a network of private, unregulated residential programs that some fifty thousand teens will attend each year in their parents' hopes of quelling their bad behavior. A fact I was unaware of when Elissa was first sent there, but has since come to consume me, still unable to shake the feeling that something must have happened while she was in the school's care, that the time she spent away from the world we co-inhabited, the life we seemed to share, somehow, someway, contributed to the fate that befell her within a year of graduation.

When I finally arrived at Ponca Pines, the school had long since closed, but I was happy to discover I could still walk freely around the fields of sun-bleached grass Elissa had once traversed. I envisioned Elissa everywhere: in the campus's abandoned, untouched stretch of buildings, painted in a coat of white so old that it was peeling off in sheaths; sitting on the wraparound porch of the residence, or beneath its sloped roof, which gives the house the appearance of a ski chalet; hanging out alongside the other classmates of hers whose lives had also come to consume me: two girls uncannily named Alyssa and Alissa.

I first discovered Alyssa and Alissa on Elissa's Facebook page; in the days after she died I'd taken to her profile with a fury—looking for solace in the litany of pictures, prayers, and memories that had come to populate her wall—but all I could focus on were the messages from Alyssa and Alissa. Messages like *Elissa taught me what it was really like to have a best friend...Love you always Elissa. Save our souls.*

Save our souls. The first time I glimpsed the phrase was on Elissa's body when she showed me the tattoo she'd gotten shortly after leaving Ponca Pines: those three words penned on her ribs in a Comic Sans–esque font. Then I saw the phrase again on Alyssa's and Alissa's bodies. *Save our souls* inked in cursive on the outside of Alyssa's left hip, and stretched across Alissa's back, horizontally, over a broken heart with angel wings. The eerie expression deepened my fascination with the girls. And by 2019, you could call it an obsession. By that year, both of their walls had also become memorial pages. Alyssa passed away at twenty-three, and Alissa died four years later, at twenty-six.

Elissa, Alyssa, Alissa, and I were all the same age, and all born into similar circumstances. We lived in suburban communities and were raised by parents with means and access. The four of us all started acting out in middle school and high school. Smoking weed, drinking, dabbling in pills. Rebellious behaviors that were of the socially acceptable, suburban variety—until they became something greater, more fearful. Considering this, I started to wonder, *Why are these girls no longer here? Why am I the one left telling this story?*

The Elissas is a look at my journey of trying to grapple with how our lives could have gone in such radically different directions. In writing it, I've interviewed more than sixty people in relation to the girls. I've spoken to those who represent the many facets of the Troubled Teen Industry. Students who feel as if the industry made a positive impact upon them, as well as those who identify as survivors and allege that they suffered abuse and neglect at these programs. Practitioners of these programs, as well as experts, journalists, and community advocates who research the effects of the industry. I've talked with the girls' friends, romantic partners, classmates. Those they met in the various troubled teen institutions they attended, or the treatment programs they enrolled in once they were no longer teens. People who have recovered from their addictions, along with young adults who still actively use. I also developed relationships with their parents and families, who I've come to believe were just as much victims of this industry as their daughters were. And while some opted to remain off the record, they still supplied me with notes about the girls' lives.

When I finally set out to write this book and tell their story, I knew I couldn't do it without resolving something in me: I had to see the Ponca Pines campus. Though it closed in 2012, there are many other institutions around the world like it, and I was still hungry to inhabit the space. Going there called to me, as if I could breathe Elissa's recycled air.

While there, I sat on the swing set where the girls would convene to gossip. There were six swings in total—three were low-hanging ones and another three sat about a foot higher off the ground—all of which gently rocked back and forth to the rhythm of the air. I gravitated to a lower one, and as I started swinging on it, all I could think about was an imagined retort from Elissa. *You're such a pussy, Sami,* she'd tease after inevitably taking a higher swing. I thought about what Elissa, Alyssa, and Alissa must've looked like on the swing set together. Picturing the girls laughing loudly, in motion, the words started coming to me. Sketching them into a scene I could already see in my head, I kept pumping, smiling, gripping the chains. Going higher and higher in the air.

CHAPTER I

Elissa

There wasn't anything I wouldn't do for Elissa, and she knew it.

We'd met when we were merely a few months old, and even in the early years, our friendship consisted of an endless onslaught of compromises. Elissa: Scheming up some elaborate act of debauchery. Me: Objecting, then relenting.

When we were in seventh grade, Elissa promised an older boy a topless photo. Selfies didn't exist yet, so she invited me over to play photographer. At first, I denied her request, fearful of the ramifications. But another, more mortifying emotion came to drown out my apprehension: jealousy. Boys never asked me for nudes. Through helping with Elissa's photo shoot, I'd become a phantom limb in the frame, basking in the warmth of the attention she received from boys by proxy. So we set to work on securing the perfect shot.

Elissa's bedroom walls were painted a pale violet, a color not unlike the faint purple veins that crisscrossed the paper-thin skin of her legs. Leaning against one such wall—triumphantly bare-chested, although quite small-breasted—Elissa instructed me how to best capture her form with my pink Motorola Razr flip phone.

"Go a little bit more from above."

"Let's try one where I'm not smiling."

"Take one with my face cut off."

Elissa was a master of her self-image, having coveted it and scrutinized it since we were in fifth grade. Growing up, she had always been a tomboy. Her hair was sheared in a brown Peter Pan–like pixie cut and her wardrobe consisted of oversized give-away T-shirts, athletic shorts, and hand-me-downs from her older brother. She was a lanky child who loved cartwheels and showing off how fast she could run. For a long time, she was grateful to her body for its gifts of speed and flexibility—never considering its flaws. Then fifth grade came, and its flaws were all she could see.

In fifth grade, Elissa came over and we spent the afternoon examining ourselves in my bathroom mirror. My childhood home had been built in the 1940s and many of the bathrooms received face-lifts in the 1970s. Mine was tiled over in a kitschy mint-green color. Everything from the floors to the ceiling, all the same shade. My mother hadn't done much to refurbish the bathroom, but she'd plastered on a cheerful wallpaper to offset the aggressive tiling. It displayed a series of half-girl/half-flowers. A violet with a smiling child's torso appearing in the pistil, legs sprouting out of the lower petals. When I looked in the mirror I mimicked their expression, smiling with full teeth.

But Elissa wasn't smiling. Her parents had recently separated;

mine had the year prior. What Elissa and I first bonded over was our on-the-surface sameness. A sisterhood built on being born and raised in the suburbs of Rhode Island, going to the same private school, the same temple, and the same country club. When our parents divorced in tandem, it didn't feel like a crazy coincidence. It was just the natural order of things, yet another experience for Elissa and me to share.

It was Elissa who clued me in on whom my father had started dating after my parents' divorce. One day, while hanging on the monkey bars, she whispered to me, I saw your dad and Auntie Becs holding hands. Rebecca was Elissa's aunt through marriage, and the mother of Faye, Shoshanna, and Zach: the three other kids who filled out our group. Rebecca was also a friend of my mother's. Before my parents' divorce, we'd all gone on shopping trips to Boston together and played at one another's houses. After, I only saw Rebecca on the Wednesday nights and alternating weekends that I spent with my dad.

Other than the hand-holding comment, Elissa and I rarely spoke of our parents' divorces. I internalized it, developing a crippling case of anxiety. Elissa became solely focused on the external: her outward appearance and how it would appeal to the opposite sex. That day in the mirror—and for years to come—she prattled on about her physical shortcomings. Her nose, which in high school she'd go on to have fixed via rhinoplasty, was much too large. Her hair was too dull, freckles too pronounced.

"We're the ugly girls, Sami," she said.

The thought had never occurred to me, but if Elissa was ugly, of course I was too. I nodded in response, paralyzed by her pronouncement. Elissa's raucous nature was alluring, but it also overwhelmed me. I locked eyes with myself in the mirror and noticed how pronounced my cheeks became when I smiled, how my stomach protruded beneath my T-shirt. I bit my cheeks and sucked in my belly as Elissa continued to list her physical flaws.

"Boys don't like ugly girls," she said while looking at us in the mirror.

"Oh," was all I could muster before the weight of her words rendered me silent for a second time.

She kept repeating the word, *ugly*, like naming it would take away its power over us. I knew less about ugly and more about beauty. Beauty was something my mother had in spades, but she'd still become depressive and despondent after the divorce. Beauty, as far as I could tell, didn't exempt you from any of life's hardships. But in Elissa's mind, beauty equaled absolution. That's what society had instructed her, anyway. As we contorted ourselves to exaggerate our greatest insecurities, Elissa spoke about beauty and boys in a way she never had before. She spoke about them with the language of desire.

Like many young women who grow up ingesting the detritus of our culture's obsession with attractive women, Elissa bought into the false promise that good looks would grant her immunity from her inner, unspoken pain. Poor little rich girls like Paris Hilton and Nicole Richie were just beginning to dominate the tabloids. In 2007, *Newsweek* conducted a poll that found that 77 percent of Americans believed women like Paris had too much influence on young girls. And in the case of Elissa and me, they were right. Their bodies, bank accounts, and bad behavior beckoned to us.

We misinterpreted the headlines that mocked their sex tapes and arrests as sheer, unadulterated praise. How could you be pretty, rich, and unhappy? Impossible. Elissa had the wealth, now she just needed to become desirable. That would solve everything.

"I want to be a slut," she told me while standing in front of my childhood bathroom mirror. It was the first time she said it but wouldn't be the last. Again, I nodded.

The following year, in sixth grade, Elissa wasn't quite ready to make good on her promise to become a slut, but she was eager to explore the more benign implications of the title. We were both spending our March vacation in Florida visiting our grandparents, and while we'd always intended to spend time together in the Sunshine State, it wasn't until then that our best-laid plans came to fruition.

My grandparents lived in Palm Beach Gardens, an expanse of gated golf communities and gussied-up strip malls. Elissa's grandparents lived on the other side of the bridge, in the ritzier, more elite Palm Beach proper. That spring break it was my father's turn to take my sister, Jordan, and me, and instead of "slumming it" at my grandmother's relatively modest winter home, he had booked a stay at The Breakers: a Renaissance Revival–style luxury hotel that had been an institution on the island since the late 1800s. My father, Douglas, was a bit of a showboat—a medical malpractice lawyer who spent more of the workweek on the golf course than in the courthouse—and The Breakers' grandiose stature suited his sensibilities.

The one thing my father wasn't, as he often lamented, was a member of the LSC: "the Lucky Sperm Club." He'd grown up with money, sure, but not the generational kind of wealth that Elissa's family—whose patriarch had been a luggage entrepreneur—was born into. When I finally visited her grandparents' ostentatious waterfront home that vacation, all I could hear were the letters *LSC* ringing in my head.

Upon arrival, I was guided to the outdoor patio to meet Elissa. Taking in their perfectly heated pool looking out on the family's private stake of the Atlantic, I couldn't have felt further away from my grandparents' community pool, where you had to go early to reserve seats and contend with swarms of hungry Jews for the best of the lunch buffet. Seeing me, Elissa shot up. Her family kept a tidy and orderly home, one Elissa was always eager to escape.

"Palm," she shouted, a nickname she'd given me for my love of chicken parm and my frequent visits to the Palm Beach area.

"Ivy," I just as energetically shouted. She wore an Allen Iverson basketball jersey nearly every day of fourth grade, and though she'd since traded athletic garb for Abercrombie miniskirts, *Ivy* had stuck.

"SLEK," we cheered in unison as we embraced, repeatedly exclaiming the combination of our initials, which we'd temporarily tattoo on our wrists in pen during math class.

Elissa hurried to collect her belongings. As she packed, I scanned her three siblings luxuriating in the ocean breeze. She was the second oldest and was close with each of them. Seth: her older, nerdier brother, whom she always included, both on her childhood playdates and on teenage party outings. Colin: her younger brother, who traveled in a pack of boys that Elissa would endlessly entertain on their nights sleeping at the family house.

Sarah: the youngest, who in her youth had a fiery streak that Elissa both revered and encouraged. On the patio, the three of them all busied themselves with different activities—swimming in the pool, walking down to the ocean—at ease amid the ostentatiousness.

Back at home the differences in our socioeconomic status were subtly omnipresent, but in Florida they were overstated and obvious. Elissa lived directly on Blackstone Boulevard, the pinnacle of Providence living. My house was just a stone's throw away from the boulevard in Pawtucket: a less prestigious province known for its lower taxes and more diverse population.

Though I never went without, I never felt totally at ease with my family's financial situation. My dad drove a Porsche, took us on trips to places like The Breakers, and belonged to multiple country clubs. But there always seemed to be a stack of bills on the island in our kitchen, with the words *Past Due* typed out in a bolded font. Whenever I'd listen in on my parents' fights, my mom would be crying about money. And that day at Elissa's grandparents' house confirmed everything I'd suspected about her family. Their wealth was real; it had roots.

There were elements of my life that she desired, too. Elissa's grandmother, the heiress to the luggage empire, kept a watchful eye over her children. She controlled the family trust, and so controlled them. To the adults, Elissa's wily demeanor wasn't charming or precocious—it was worrisome, something to curb. My family had far fewer rules, which Elissa and I exploited, constantly. Our day at The Breakers was no exception.

Once back at the hotel, my father established himself poolside, lathering his leathery body in an SPF 5 oil. My sister, Jordan, who was seven, hung behind with him. He was the only single father there—though he wasn't truly single—a status he exulted in, using it to flirt with eligible passersby. The rest of the sun worshippers, by and large, were all families who had flown in from posher East Coast suburbs like Fairfield and Westchester Counties. Come summer, they all flocked to the same locales: Nantucket, the Hamptons, Martha's Vineyard. Packs of chummy, moneyed families playing musical pool chairs, in one luxe locale after another.

None of it interested Elissa or me, so we made our way to the hotel's "kids' club": a small, house-like building with a variety of billiards and arcade games designated for the young patrons. To Elissa and me, it was Bungalow 8, but in reality, it was nothing more than an elevated rec room. Elissa had a nose for sniffing out boys. While she still wasn't exactly beautiful, she'd grown out her hair and purchased a push-up bra. We both watched *The Simple Life* religiously and treated our viewings like finishing school: Elissa mastered Paris Hilton's baby-voiced, come-hither demeanor while I studied Nicole Richie's sarcastic, sardonic schtick. Back at the kids' club, it didn't take long for Elissa to find Wyatt and Archie, two polo-shirted unwitting tweens, for us to try out our Paris and Nicole routine on. Wyatt had shaggy, surfer blond hair and Archie kept his in the properly clipped cut of an older man. Neither of us was particularly attracted to them, but it didn't matter. They were science experiments, not suitors.

"How far have you gone?" It was one of Elissa's favorite questions to ask, immediately disarming any twelve-year-old who dared to enter her orbit. Wyatt and Archie shifted in their loafers, uneasy in their lack of experience. At that point, Elissa was also inexperienced, but her chutzpah made up for her never-been-kissed status.

"Ummm," Wyatt began to respond, making it clear that I wasn't the only one Elissa could silence.

Before they could volley the question back to her, Elissa was on to her next mind game. A hallmark of *The Simple Life* was Paris and Nicole's shared love of hijinks. The deliberately ditzy twosome was always cooking up some sort of ruse to unnerve the "real Americans" they encountered in their travels. After Elissa, Wyatt, Archie, and I took turns playing Pac-Man, she decided it was time to pull a prank of our own. Elissa and I would go to the hotel gift shop and purchase a pack of condoms. Not for sex, not yet. In sixth grade it was about the thrill of anything that suggested sex. The word alone sent shivers up our spines.

The Breakers had a stretch of storefronts surrounding the main entrance. A Lilly Pulitzer store for moms and daughters. A Polo Ralph Lauren for fathers and sons. The Signature Shop was where you could purchase travel-sized Kiehl's products, tees and totes with the resort's label, and luckily for us, condoms. We spotted them quickly but took our time scanning the aisles, to appear "discreet." The waiting weighed on me the most. I ran my finger-tips against The Breakers' emblazoned glassware, La Roche-Posay sunscreen, and Acqua di Parma fragrances as I ran through the list of possible outcomes for our actions. *Is there an age require-ment for buying condoms?* I wondered. *You have to be eighteen for cigarettes and lottery tickets, but condoms?* Elissa's overly excited, darting eyes snapped me back into the present.

"I'll bring them to the counter, but you have to give your room number," she told me.

"Fine," I conceded.

That was the extent of our plan. Elissa made her way to the counter first, and as she threw a pack of gum in with the condoms, I choked out a quiet declaration of the junior suite we were staying in. The male cashier surveyed the two twelve-year-old, Juicy Couture–clad girls in front of him. We looked every bit the part of a Breakers hotel guest, down to our unshakable air of entitlement. He had at least twenty years on us, but we were the guests and that status meant he completed the transaction, no questions asked. While he put the Trojans into a plastic bag, I attempted to maintain my composure as a wave of exhilaration spread through my body. My worry had transmuted itself into elation.

"Told you it'd be fine," she said.

"That was crazy," I replied breathlessly.

Elissa's on-the-surface attitude was blasé, but her eager eyes betrayed her true emotions. She was fucking thrilled. Wyatt and Archie waited for us outside the shop—not even playing lookout, just barely curious bystanders. When we rejoined them, they appeared more shocked than stoked by our bounty. Our success presented a new challenge: What would we do with the condoms?

"What are you thinking?" Wyatt asked, mainly looking at Elissa.

"I have some ideas," she said, casually buying time.

At that age we were always teetering on the edge of true rebellion. We snorted Pixy Stix, pretending the powder was cocaine. We burned incense, acting as if the fumes were pot. When we got back to the kids' club, we decided to make condom water balloons. The four of us hovered around a sink in the girls' room, filling each plastic casing with lukewarm tap water. I'd never seen a condom in person before and I marveled at the different shapes they formed. One, growing wide and circular like a silicone breast implant. Another, becoming long and narrow, like the limp limb of a balloon animal. Once done, we lifted our shirts, cradling our creations in the fabric as we migrated to the secluded area behind the kids' club. There was nothing to do but throw them on the ground. Elissa wound up like a pitcher taking the mound, cranking her arm around again and again, trying to rev up the most centrifugal force. I stood on my tiptoes, lifting my hand as far into the sky as I could possibly get it, hoping to access more of gravity's power. Then we let it rip.

"Holy shit. Holy shit," Elissa and I both screamed.

The balloons cannonballed, splashing water and latex onto The Breakers' redbrick-lined grounds. We were giddy and glowing, screaming *again, again, again* as we threw every one of those condoms smack against the now-desecrated courtyard. With each toss we thought less about appearing cool to the boys. Soon, we forgot they were even there. We were besotted in our girlish abandon; nobody existed outside of us.

That was the thing about being friends with Elissa. I had to understand that there was no pleasure without pain. That the further she pushed my elastic limits, the more outsized the reward. The more uncomfortable she made me feel, the more fun we'd have in the end.

It wasn't until seventh grade—the year of the naked photos—that Elissa's self-fulfilling prophecy of becoming a slut would truly begin to calcify, and her rebellious streak would begin in earnest. Poor little rich girls don't just wake up one day fully formed, ready to denounce the patriarchal and privileged order that they were born into in the name of a good time. It starts as a ringing, nearly imperceptible at first, that grows louder and louder until it's impossible to ignore. While I never quite heard it, I've come to realize that this ringing is the realization that life among the cohorts at the country club is not all that you were told it would be. It's the mounting rejection of the slow march toward becoming your mother, to marrying a type like your father, to putting out carbon copies of yourself that one day will also dine at the same country club, commingling with the same cohorts.

Rebellion becomes a mold you can pour yourself into, modeling your behavior on the glamorous portrayals of poor little rich girls before you. The fictional ones like Lux Lisbon, Daisy Buchanan, Marissa Cooper. Or the ingenues so mythologized, they feel like characters: Edie Sedgwick, Peaches Geldof, Paris. White women have an experience of being a teenager that's in total opposition to that of young girls of color, whom society views as adults from the onset.[1] Robbing them of their innocence at the first chance. Instead, these poor little rich girls experience a youth so romanticized, its lure is undeniable. There's a cost to joining this lineage—and sometimes it's the ultimate price.

In sixth grade, Elissa was just beginning to hear the ringing. The danger was still to come.

CHAPTER II

Alyssa

From the moment I discovered Alyssa, I was excruciatingly envious of her relationship with Elissa. The two met when they were roommates at Ponca Pines, and the connection between them was immediate—a bond based on the shared pronunciation of their names, being raised in our Jewish, upper-middle-class milieu, and each harboring an unruly obsession with boys. But whereas Elissa cast a wide net—commanding the attention of everyone she encountered—Alyssa's desires were singular. Or, to put it how they would: Elissa was a slut and Alyssa was a boyfriend girl.

Growing up in Northbrook, Illinois, Alyssa had been a slouchy, submissive girl who ripped her sandwiches into pieces throughout a meal, too anxious to take a bite. A people pleaser by nature, she looked to those around her to make her whole. She'd had a few boyfriends who temporarily flooded the levee to that vacant part of her being. But when she met Owen, the dam was destroyed. His love runneth over.

Owen, for his part, was a dime-bag, small-time drug dealer, a distinction that made him irrelevant in the eyes of the law, but an outlaw to the high schoolers who kept his business afloat. It's easy for these types of pot pushers to take on a mystical quality to their more naive patrons. To contact them requires a friend to vouch for a friend who's been previously vouched for by another friend. They don't text in legible sentences, rather in a poorly crafted secret language where "Christmas tree" means weed and "Megan Fox" stands for cocaine. Their existence is confined to the shadows of abandoned parking lots and alleyways. When they cast their gaze on you, it's electrifying.

In Providence, our Owen stand-in was Auggie, a boy Elissa knew from her childhood Little League team who smoked us out with our first joint in the same dugout where they'd met as kids. A couple of years later, after Elissa was sent to Nebraska, Auggie and I reconnected at a party where he punched my classmate and then ushered me out back to smoke a Marlboro Red. Everybody loves the quarterback until they meet the bad boy.

"Hey," was the first word Owen ever spoke to Alyssa. Though the two had never met, mutual friends had invited Alyssa to go hang in Owen's unfinished attic. When she arrived, Owen realized how badly he wanted to get to know her.

"Hey," Alyssa echoed.

"Smoke?" he asked.

"For sure," she replied.

"Word," Owen said, ushering Alyssa into his room.

Owen didn't know it, but the square shape of Alyssa's childhood frame had only recently contorted itself into the curved figure before him. She'd lengthened and thinned, becoming a skinny teen girl of above-average height. Only her breasts retained the weight she'd lost. Alyssa had the kind of disproportionately Barbie-esque breasts that feminist parents warn their daughters about, telling them that if a woman actually had the doll's chest, she'd keel over under the sheer mass. Owen wasn't the first boy to notice them. Her breasts beckoned to her high school class-mates. She was everything teen movies had taught boys about a girl's experience of puberty—that overnight, the ugly duckling will sprout double Ds and transform from an innocent outcast to a fully sexualized woman, ready for the taking.

It wasn't just the boys who objectified Alyssa. She could do that all on her own. While Alyssa had the biological gift of hot-ness that Elissa and I aspired to, she still had to learn to play the part. Teen girls are taught that there's no greater achieve-ment than being hot. It's a term so ubiquitous that Paris Hilton even used it as a stamp of approval, declaring of anything cool, good, or worthy, "That's hot." In the 2005 book *Female Chauvinist Pigs: Women and the Rise of Raunch Culture*, journalist Ariel Levy explores how being called hot was an entirely different distinction from being recognized as beautiful or attractive. Instead, it was rooted in the fuckability and salability of your body. In order to achieve this status, Alyssa fashioned herself in tight, low-cut tops and corresponding low-rise jeans, flatironing her dark brown hair and tracing her lower eyelids in smudgy black circles. She stopped hunching in the hallways and began performing the role of the hot girl, now strutting through them.

Self-objectification is a rite of womanhood, but it's an exhausting one. Suddenly you're overcome by a quiet yet constant reevaluation of how your body looks at any given moment. As Elissa instructed me that day in the mirror, your body isn't a whole, but a collection of worrisome parts. At any given moment your arms can look too fat, your thigh gap too narrow, your breasts not perky enough. Every reflective surface becomes a tool for self-examination, an outlet to pick your body apart as you ready it to be perceived by boys, girls, adults, fellow teens. Girls aren't discriminatory when it comes to approval.

In Peggy Orenstein's 2016 *Girls & Sex: Navigating the Complicated New Landscape*, she warns, "Self-objectification has been associated with depression, reduced cognitive function, lower GPA, distorted body image, body monitoring, eating disorders, risky sexual behavior, and reduced sexual pleasure." But Alyssa's self-objectification also came with a fresh set of privileges: attention from boys; envy from girls. What she prized above all else was her acceptance into Glenbrook North High School's fast crowd, the type of blissfully invincible weed-smoking, class-cutting, pill-popping group that seems to exist at every high school, in every community, in every upper-middle-class part of the country. The type that Elissa would come to seek out once our friendship started to fall apart. Alyssa met Owen in that crowd.

"Can I get your number?" he asked after they rejoined the kickback. He could have just as easily asked for her Facebook page, or her BBM account. The late 2000s were all about poking, pinging, and any other form of digital prodding.

"Sure," she said.

Many people I have spoken with about Owen describe him

as an ominous, fear-invoking figure—referring to him as a dirt-bag they felt afraid to speak about on the record. Owen himself declined my many requests to speak. But Alyssa had no such fear of him. She took him in as he appeared, reputation aside. To her he was just a tall twenty-year-old with a muscular build and a swoosh of black hair that seemed to perfectly offset his pale blue eyes. The pulsing, electromagnetic current also known as mutual attraction charged their shared gaze, and one thing was clear: Owen had Alyssa, hook, line, and sinker.

"See you around," Owen said.

"Bye," was all she could muster.

One of the first people Alyssa told about Owen was Morgan, a fellow member of Glenbrook's fast crowd whom Alyssa had been close friends with since elementary school, back when Alyssa's shyness rendered her invisible, her self-consciousness overshadowing her natural good looks. A core pillar of their friendship had always been that sharing was caring. In sixth grade, Alyssa—who was considerably more wealthy than Morgan—would give Morgan her hand-me-downs. Come junior year, they started to split Alyssa's ADHD meds. Once Owen became Alyssa's boyfriend, she found a way for Morgan to partake in her newfound joy: a setup with Owen's best friend, Tyler.

The four started spending their days in that ramshackle room above Owen's parents' garage, taking turns making out on the futon, smoking Owen's stash, and playing with his heterochromic dog. Alyssa, who had always felt uneasy in her own skin, was now awash in pheromones, THC, and a feeling of acceptance. For teen girls, it's often not about who this almighty, all-encompassing boyfriend actually is, but rather how said boyfriend makes them feel—and saddled up next to Owen in his low-rent love shack, Alyssa felt like her life had locked into place. Whether or not she could sense it at the time, these unfettered afternoons in the attic became the pinnacle of Alyssa's existence. The rest of her life unspooled like a never-ending state of withdrawal, a constant aching for that first hit of first love.

To the outside observer, namely, Alyssa's mother, her life was taking a turn for the worse. By the time that Alyssa met Owen she'd already received many diagnoses: social anxiety, depression, ADHD. Alyssa's father, Richard, was a neurologist and her mother, Louise, a believer in the merits of therapy. She spent Alyssa's teen years taking her to various psychologists. Therapy is fairly commonplace in communities like Northbrook, especially as mental illness has become one of the greatest risks facing teenagers today. While three decades ago, binge-drinking, drunk driving, teen pregnancy, and the like posed the biggest threats to teenagers, in the intervening years these dangers have been replaced by anxiety, depression, suicide, and self-harm.[1] But no matter how many therapists Alyssa saw, the conclusion remained the same: It was impossible to demolish the wall Alyssa put up.

Alyssa had been erecting this wall brick by brick throughout her Northbrookian childhood. During it, Northbrook had transformed into a behemoth full of modern McMansions, but Alyssa's family and their modest, medium-sized home evoked the era that immortalized the community. The John Hughes era. When *The Breakfast Club* filmmaker was a teen, his family decamped to

Northbrook. An outsider looking in, he became infatuated with the town: its quintessentially North Shore charm; its striving, upwardly mobile population. Though his '80s high school dramedies are set in the fictional "Shermer, Illinois," Northbrook's sensibilities persist on-screen. His films showcase the community's well-to-do, white public schools filled with middle-of-the-pack, upper-middle-class teens prone to the kind of debauchery to which adults offer a knowing wink. All these overtly romantic trappings came to populate Shermer: a suburb spectacular only in its ordinariness.

Alyssa had the makings of a Hughesian heroine. She wasn't a Northbrook transplant; she and her older brother, Eli, were born and raised in the town and thus afforded all the privileges the zip code provides. Sports leagues, summer camps, a stable family, the works. But like Molly Ringwald's characters before her, Alyssa's innately anxious, sensitive disposition made her an outsider despite her access to the inside. What complicated matters was just how aware Alyssa was of these shortcomings.

The one place Alyssa felt comfortable being herself was the summer camp she went to with her childhood best friend, Kate. When I talk with Kate—who's now an elementary school teacher in a suburb not far from Northbrook—I have to stop myself from projecting too much. There's much about Alyssa's childhood I've come to identify with. Her family's Judaism, their standing in the community. But it's Kate whom I feel connected to within Alyssa's greater story. Kate's family is friends with Alyssa's, and as children they did everything together, even throwing joint birthday parties. They only grew apart when Alyssa began gravitating toward Glenbrook's fast crowd, with Kate hanging back, uninterested and uninvited by that scene.

What also resonates with me is the tinge of survivor's guilt that I detect in Kate's voice. I first discovered the term while watching *Ordinary People*, the story of two brothers, the older of whom drowns during a sailing accident, with the younger plagued by such regret and PTSD that he attempts to take his own life. For a long time, I didn't feel worthy of the term *survivor's guilt*. Like it was something reserved for someone in the kind of pain that would drive them to suicide. Not for someone like me, whose pain mostly comes at night, when I dream that Elissa has come back to life only to die again, this time right in front of me, leading me to wake up, shaky and sticky and rattled by the injustice of the fact that I'm here and she's not.

As we continue to talk, Kate prefers to focus on the before times. Like how much Alyssa loved summer camp, allowing herself to be the loudmouthed, goofy version of Alyssa so few got to see. Or the night that she sat with Kate by the campfire, crying and talking about how she knew exactly the way she presented to those around her—cripplingly shy and closed off—she just didn't know how to stop herself from behaving that way. A rare admission for Alyssa, who preferred to keep her emotions closed off, and just for herself. Until she met Owen and invited him behind the wall.

Owen became Alyssa's version of the coping mechanism girls have employed since the beginning of time. The more therapists who passed her off, and the more that unknown, unspeakable pain of hers went silenced, the more having a boyfriend became the salve. Society teaches young women that locking down a man is the ultimate aim. So why, then, wouldn't girls believe that burrowing themselves into a boyfriend will balance out all the bad? While Owen's appearance in Alyssa's life signaled the beginning of the end, his arrival was far from the start. Alyssa's grades had faltered since puberty. She'd dabbled with drugs since freshman year and truancy had long been an issue. Then once she started dating Owen, it got worse.

With a 96 percent graduation rate, and a record-high ranking as the forty-eighth-best public high school in the country, Glenbrook wasn't a place to let its students fall by the wayside. Its educators were committed to finding an equitable solution to Alyssa's attendance problem. Their student body hovered around two thousand kids: Each mattered when it came to maintaining their exemplar statistics. Alyssa mattered. Glenbrook agreed to let Alyssa take online classes and when she refused to complete them, they referred her to a local hospital with an outpatient program for students who stopped attending school due to anxiety. If you can afford the price, there is always a solution, some treatment, an alternative program for suburban parents to enroll their child in. Each offers the impossibly attractive promise of returning a child to the righteous path. This outpatient treatment center in town was the first to offer Alyssa's family that promise.

"When I went to pick her up the first day, the therapist called me into her office and told me they had drug tested her and found very high levels of THC in her blood," Louise writes to me now.

The revelation surprised her. Louise knew what a high person looked like. She'd gone to college. She wasn't a square. But she couldn't seem to square Alyssa's quiet, closed-off demeanor with what she remembered of the weed smokers on her campus: the goofy, giggling potheads with their liberal sensibilities and their turn on, tune in, drop out attitudes. Stoners behaved like Spicoli or Cheech & Chong. Not like her baby girl.

Taking in the therapist's comments, Louise allowed herself a moment to reflect on her daughter's behavior of late. The defiance, the disinterest in her education, the all-consuming quality of her latest relationship. Ever since Alyssa's body had developed, her interest in dating outweighed every other sector of life. There was Colin: the nice enough, skateboarder-looking classmate of Alyssa's who had escorted her to a school dance. Alyssa had worn a bright orange, skinny-strapped dress with a hem that hovered just below her fingertips. Colin styled his shirt in an untucked fashion and paired his cargo pants with sneakers. Slovenly, but a perfectly suitable suitor. They didn't last long, and a series of short-lived flings followed, all of which were rendered unmemorable in comparison to the intensity of Alyssa's new relationship with Owen. If there was anything Alyssa seemed high on, it was Owen himself.

Why wouldn't Louise blame Owen? He was mysterious, older, and taking up all of Alyssa's attention. But in focusing on Owen himself, Louise might have been unaware of what drew Alyssa to Owen in the first place. She was right to pinpoint the reason for the change in Alyssa's behavior as her body's changes. But Alyssa's preoccupation with her body wasn't pure vanity; it was a way to self-soothe. Throughout *Girls & Sex*, Orenstein wrestles with the reasons why the young women she interviews are so fixated on making themselves look "hot." To me, the answer is obvious. We prize girls' adolescent good looks and instruct them that beauty is a fleeting gift for the young. The rituals of cultivating such beauty—maintaining an optimum weight, making over your face with makeup—become a numbing device. Like Sydney Sweeney's character in *Euphoria*, who when going through a rough patch begins waking up every morning at four a.m. to shower, scrub, shave, gua sha, and jade roll before school. These routines become something for girls like Alyssa to focus on instead of the mess of their minds. And when a boy notices these efforts, it's the ultimate form of validation.

"The therapist told me they could only continue to work with her if she was admitted to inpatient psych. She said that another alternative would be sending Alyssa to a wilderness program. She gave me the name of an 'educational consultant' who could find a program for her. This was our entry into the Troubled Teen Industry," Louise says of how the rest of their conversation followed.

Wilderness program: The term was foreign to Louise. Like it was to Elissa's mother before she sent Elissa to the one in Montana. Louise would soon learn that the wilderness is the gateway to the Troubled Teen Industry, a web of therapeutic boarding schools, boot camps, and other treatment centers that preach tough love and practice behavior modification.

The typical length of a wilderness program stay is two to three months, a period spent traversing various trails with a small group of similarly struggling teens. These programs sell themselves on outdoor therapy sessions, bonding exercises, and communal sharing over nightly campfires. What they don't publicize is the federal report that was issued in 2007, investigating the cases of ten teen-agers who died while in wilderness programs. The report included evidence that some teenagers were starved and made to eat dirt or their own vomit. It also found "significant evidence of ineffective management" and "reckless or negligent operating practices."[2]

"I met with the educational consultant. She asked a few ques-tions about Alyssa and recommended a few programs. She never met with Alyssa. Since it was February and we couldn't stand the thought of sending her into the woods we picked a program in Hawaii called Pacific Quest. It was breathtakingly expensive but we were desperate," Louise says.

The question that still remains for me is why was one day in the outpatient program's care—and one failed drug test—enough to deem Alyssa unsuitable for treatment? Why was this therapist yet another one in the long line of medical professionals who only saw Alyssa's prickly exterior, unwilling to do the work to get at what the wall was erected to protect?

If Louise hadn't been encouraged to make the agonizing choice to send her daughter away, maybe Alyssa's relationship with Owen would've simply run its course. Perhaps when Alyssa discovered that Owen was using heroin, that would've been the nail in the coffin of their courtship—not the introduction of a thrilling new chapter. But in her anger at her family for shipping her off, and her distrust in the professionals who encouraged it, Alyssa started to see Owen as her salvation. She immortalized him as the one person who made her feel loved, before he was ripped away from her. Owen became a false god, a symbol of the acceptance she so craved that she would fight to return to it no matter where the Troubled Teen Industry took her, no matter the consequence.

Within a few weeks Alyssa was on a plane to Pacific Quest. The promotional materials for the program made it easy to get swept up in its ocean views. How the slow rocking of the Pacific's waves would lull Alyssa to sleep at night. Peaceful, content.

CHAPTER III

Alissa

Ponca Pines Academy typically enrolled only twelve or so girls at a time, priding themselves on their small classes and the intimate nature of their schooling. While Elissa was in attendance, the majority of the school's dozen-odd students bore either the same or strikingly similar names. Like Allie and Ali, along with Halle. Of course, there were the one-offs: a Charlotte, a Hannah. But there were also Elissa, Alyssa, and Alissa.

Alissa grew up in Omaha, Nebraska, where she was every bit the baby of her family. Her mother and father, Claire and John, had their children in pairs. First came Mary and Matt, born in quick succession. A decade later, Claire gave birth to her second set—Brian and Alissa—and their family was made whole.

Being born last lent a feeling of stasis to Alissa's childhood, an innocence that lingered into her early teen years. As a consequence of her birth order, she was spoiled. By Mary, who behaved like her second mother, often instructing her in the room they shared. By her father, whose favorite form of paternal bonding was taking Alissa to the mall. The indulgences planted a stubbornness in Alissa, one her family teased would rear its head in a fashion similar to that of the donkey in *Shrek*. Ironically, these slight shortcomings only made her family members coddle and covet her all the more.

Then her childhood ended. Claire and John had been married for thirty-two years when they announced their separation. A lover of traditions, Alissa became fixated on what Christmas would look like: fretting over whether or not they'd still have their annual cookie-baking competition. The last traces of her prolonged naivete shielded Alissa from noticing the larger, more consequential changes that were coming her way. Like that her father would retain their childhood home and her relationship with him would be forever altered.

Daddy issues: a sensation that I know well, despite how different Alissa's father is from mine. Alissa's dad is a quiet, reserved man. Mine has the boisterous energy of a former frat star, though he never pledged. As far back as I can remember, Thursday nights were my dad's night out. He'd spend them at our country club, playing a round of golf before retiring to the locker room, where he'd spend the rest of the evening playing gin rummy. I loved my dad's standing at our country club. He was one of the best golfers, and when he competed in the annual club championship, he'd let me tag along and watch. I felt like the mayor's daughter, as if popularity was in my blood.

After my parents got divorced, he started spending more and more time at the club. Sometimes, on the nights he was supposed to take my sister and me to dinner, he'd disappear there, not answering my calls until I'd get in touch with the pro shop, having the cashier go and find him and hand him the phone. Even though I always knew, deep down, that he was just back in the locker room, I could never stop myself from getting worked up when he'd vanish. Crying and imagining his car turned over in a ditch, or a sand trap.

It's a cliché to say that daddy issues are often the subconscious impetus for young women to act out, but for Alissa the change in her behavior seemed to coincide with the change in her relationship with her father. Claire was now working long hours as a medication aide in a retirement home, and Alissa grew fond of her newfound freedom living alone with her mom. She called dibs on the lone bedroom in the finished basement. The space had its own bathroom, hangout area, and most importantly, a private entrance to the home. Claire furnished it with a couch and a television and soon Alissa and her girlfriends were spending full weekends down below, only coming aboveground to replenish their snack stash.

"What's left of the Malibu?" Amy asked while Alissa fiddled with the liquor bottles they'd slowly been accumulating over the past few months, hiding them in various crevices of the basement.

"I think we drained most of it," Alissa replied, crouching to look at how much liquid was left in the bottle the way she'd been instructed to read the contents of a beaker in chemistry class.

"You think there's enough to get us shwaaaasted?" Lily asked.

"Worth a shot."

"Wait, should we take shots?"

"Oh my god. Fuck yes."

She was now living outside the neighborhood she'd been raised in and working for the first time, waitressing at Red Robin to pay for the car she used to shuttle herself to class. But Amy and Lily offered Alissa a constant that she didn't have in her family life. Lily was a year older and had met Alissa through the cheerleading they both participated in. Alissa had known Amy since she was a kid, and ever since Amy had spent summers accompanying Alissa's family to their vacation house in Missouri, tagging along on their day trips to amusement parks, evenings spent at the bowling alley, and the occasional Sunday outing to church.

"Here," Amy said as she passed Alissa a shot.

"Do you think the gin would be, like, too vile?" Alissa asked, pulling out the next bottle.

"I mean...," Lily said, shrugging while unscrewing the cap.

"Ohmigod," Alissa said after slugging straight from the bottle. Too vile, it was not.

For girls like us, basements are the most quintessentially suburban haven for adolescent experimentation. We had a finished basement at my home, replete with an air hockey machine, foosball table, and vintage arcade games. As I got older, Elissa and I spent more time hanging out within its dark, wood-paneled confines. We huffed cleaning supplies, the first time I ever opted to deplete my own brain cells. We invited over neighborhood boys to play truth or dare, the first time I ever felt a penis. Basements are the prom night of the home: Parents know what happens in them, but most turn a blind eye when confronted with the reality. There's a certain level of experimentation that parents are instructed to stomach. A few swigs of alcohol, a couple tokes of pot. At first,

that's all it was for Alissa, Amy, and Lily. An odd night playing Russian roulette with their taste buds, seeing which types of
liquor they could swallow.

"Shit, I'm, like, *feeling* it," Amy said.

"Bottoms up, betch."

Most teens are the exception to what D.A.R.E. ads threaten:
able to smoke weed without later turning to heroin, capable of
exploring their sexuality without becoming a sex addict. And
while there's no concrete answer for what makes teens go one
way or the other, there are always certain indicators as to why a
girl like Alissa's drinking would grow to be a concern. Possibili-
ties that wouldn't become apparent until years later, when childhood trauma was declared a public health crisis. Linking what are
called adverse childhood experiences (ACEs) to smoking, alcoholism, drug abuse, depression, heart disease, lung disease, and even
cancer.[1]

Now, in the age of therapy-speak, everything is a trigger, or a
trauma, or a form of damage. Where Instagram is flooded with
infographics about ACEs, and links to quizzes to determine if
you're suffering from them. But when Alissa was in high school,
few knew to constitute her parents' divorce as an ACE. Or her
brother Matt's incarceration as one. There was little understanding that trauma was a small word with big baggage.

In response, her stubbornness transformed into a tempes-
tuousness, one that she frequently took out on Claire. Alissa
was angry that Claire left her alone so often; Claire was upset
that when she came home from a hard day's work there were so
many girls in the basement. Claire didn't trust Alissa's friends

who came and went tiptoeing through the back entrance at all hours of the day. They were cagey and prone to petty theft. But whenever Claire would try to confront Alissa about the chaos emanating from the basement, she played the ultimate trump card: *I hate being by myself and you're never here. What do you expect me to do?*

Their most explosive fights were about Alissa's body. In the 2000s our teen years lined up with a mass weight loss among Hollywood's ingenues. Nicole Richie had stepped away from *The Simple Life* and sought reinvention. The celebutante was now shedding her terry cloth two-pieces and barely there curves in an attempt to stay hip to the times. Once Elissa and I were in high school, the unmistakably thinner Richie had started working with Rachel Zoe, a stylist who pioneered "boho-chic." Mischa Barton and Lindsay Lohan also sidled up to her, dressing in looks that were all clavicle and caftan. As Zoe's clients' dress sizes dwindled, she publicly denied her role in the glorification of the size zero.[2] But no matter who was responsible, size zero became the platonic ideal of what a body should be to me and many other girls who came of age alongside me. Once, on another flight home from Palm Beach Gardens, I pored through a magazine until I landed on a collage of starlets, Hilary Duff, Mandy Moore, Mischa, Lindsay, Nicole, all with their weights listed beneath them. At first I felt comforted to see numbers that had appeared on my scale at home, low 130s. Others were in the mid-120s. Then I looked farther down. Those were the *before* numbers. None were above 112 pounds. *Could I ever have their determination?*

My nose was always stuck in a magazine. I'd borrow my mother's copies of *InStyle* and flip through the pages of red-carpet fashion galleries, memorizing the names of celebrities. By ninth grade, I'd graduated to Perez Hilton, designating his blog as the homepage on my Safari browser, spending hours scrolling through his posts on the comings and goings of Paris, Lindsay, and Nicole. And I was like a vacuum, devouring every last drop of the rehab stints, public meltdowns, breakups, and hookups—then immediately growing itchy for more.

While Alissa might not have been engaging with pop culture on quite the same level that I was, its ripples still reached her. Particularly when it came to dieting. In the early 2000s, juice cleanses were all the rage. Beyoncé had done the Master Cleanse to prepare her body for *Dreamgirls*, dropping twenty pounds by subsisting on a concoction of lemon juice, maple syrup, and cayenne pepper.[3] Alissa tried them all, and when these diets inevitably failed, she always returned to her old faithful: shunning carbs, consuming only fruits and vegetables. But no matter what she tried, still she remained an average-sized teenage girl.

"Do these jeans make my ass look fat?" Alissa asked Claire from the dressing room: the most sacred of all mother-daughter battlegrounds. Where struggles have been waged so entrenched in psychological warfare, so covertly catastrophic, waterboarding ought to be more pleasant.

"You look beautiful," Claire responded. She'd grown to dread shopping with Alissa, feeling suffocated by the fluorescent lighting and Alissa's impossible-to-answer-correctly questions.

"That's not an answer, Mom."

"I think they look great. How's that for an answer?"

"You have to say that. You're my *mom*."

Claire wasn't particularly worried about Alissa's eating habits. She'd grown up during the height of the grapefruit diet, where women ate one half of the fruit before every meal to stave off hunger. By the 1980s, women began replacing their grapefruits with beets. The Master Cleanse was just the latest iteration, another temporary fix, a Band-Aid for bad body image. While Claire was troubled by the low self-esteem Alissa had, she comforted herself with the knowledge that no woman truly has *high* self-esteem. Insecurity is the inheritance of womanhood. Does anyone look in the mirror without fantasizing about being a dress size smaller, two inches taller, having different breasts? Alissa was normal to have these feelings, Claire thought.

"Well, I don't love the stitching on them."

"I fucking knew it. You think I look fat."

"No, I don't!" Claire replied.

"Just admit it, Mom," Alissa said.

"Get them if you like them! The stitching is just a *me* thing."

"Are you kidding? I clearly look terrible in them."

"Alissa, please."

These were the types of conversations I, too, was having with my mother, in yet another dressing room, in a vastly different part of the country. Years later, on my calls with Claire, I recount these experiences for her when she describes her fights with Alissa. I also spent time with her on my trip to Nebraska, eating chicken salad sandwiches with her and Mary at an outdoor shopping mall, growing immensely fond of her in the process. I love telling her about how I'd spend hours obsessing over the way a pair of low-rise 7 For All Mankind jeans framed my hips, or how the signature cursive *A* on the pocket looked on my ass. Just one look from my mother would send us into a yelling match about whether my hips were more muffin top or hourglass. That makes Claire laugh, her low, soft laugh that radiates warmth and basks our conversations in a light that is a welcome pivot for us both as we talk of her daughter's death.

What I don't tell Claire is that I also dabbled in disordered eating in high school. Bingeing on large slices of the crispy eggplant pizza slices I liked from the pizza parlor by Wheeler, just to rid myself of them in the dining hall bathroom. The habit didn't last long—I only successfully purged the slices from my body a few times before I quit—but the desire to massacre my body in the name of weight loss never waned. To become the after in the tabloid pictures, not the before.

In Caroline Knapp's 2004 book, *Appetites: Why Women Want*, she cites a study out of the University of Cincinnati College of Medicine in which nearly thirty thousand women shared that losing weight was more important to them than any other goal. As I dig deeper into the lives of Elissa, Alyssa, and Alissa, I return to this book often, reading it with an intensity that borders on religiosity: underlining passages, cluttering the pages with marginalia, texting block quotes to my friends. Her words uncover so many of the feelings I've never been able to name, in regard to both my own life and these women's stories, making me better understand the sensation that she calls "disorders of appetite": "Food addictions, compulsive shopping, promiscuous sex—have a kind of semiotic brilliance, expressing in symbol and metaphor what women themselves may not be able to express in words," Knapp writes in *Appetites*.

It wasn't until Ponca Pines that Alissa's anorexia would truly flourish, that she'd experience this symbolic, semiotic brilliance. Where she'd learn the power such a coping mechanism provides, seeking out more and more extreme methods. Hungry for any and all relief.

CHAPTER IV

Elissa

Each suburb has its own mythology. In Providence, there seemed to be two stories told at every sleepover, every coed commingling. The first was Jolly Rancher girl. A young woman of indeterminate age who had the habit of inserting the fruit-flavored sucker into her vagina, instructing her boyfriend to fish it out while he performed oral sex on her. Then one fateful night, his tongue retrieved something else entirely. A "pus ball" the size of said Jolly Rancher. We'd pantomime gagging, scream at the story-teller to stop, then by the next hangout we'd be at it again, reciting the tale. The other myth featured a girl who decided to try anal sex for the first time. As her boyfriend pulled out, an onslaught of feces followed. Suddenly, there was shit everywhere: all over the couch, the rug, the walls. More shit than you've ever seen in your life. When her parents came home amid the cleanup, the couple scrambled, blaming the family's senior dog. In a flash, the father took the dog around back and shot him dead. The relationship, naturally, never recovered.

While someone would always inevitably claim that Jolly Rancher girl was their cousin's neighbor's best friend, or that they'd legitimately grown up with the boyfriend behind the anal sex—we never really knew where these stories came from. Or if they had any semblance of validity. But they lived on in infamy, turning their subjects into demigods. Soon, Elissa would have one all her own.

In seventh grade, Elissa still hadn't had her first kiss. Neither had I, so we'd lie around discussing the mechanics. How much tongue you should employ, what to do with your teeth, the threat of bad breath. We'd talk about other sex acts, too. Elissa and I both agreed that while we'd be willing to give a blow job, we'd never let someone go down on us. The smell, the ick of it all. *How could you ever relax into something like that?* we wondered. Fingering we could fathom—we'd both started shaving our pubes sometime that year, just in *case* someone wanted to finger us—but no way would we ever let someone put their mouth there. For a long time, just talking about sex satiated us. Words like *eating out* and *head* felt foreign and forbidden on our tongues.

"They're going to be here soon," Elissa said, referring to the three older boys she'd invited to my basement. Then she started fidgeting with her jean skirt, hiking it up higher on her hips to show more thigh.

"Did they *actually* say they were coming?" I asked. Boys were always promising Elissa things on AIM. Offline, it was another story.

"Yes, skank. He promised."

Kissing aside, Elissa had developed a bit of notoriety. At the dances, when entering the mosh pit of middle schoolers flailing their limbs to "Ms. New Booty," she'd pull her whale tail out, daring someone to grind with her. It always worked. Then those boys with whom she'd shared a dance—along with their "boys," older brothers, and distant cousins—would find her on Instant Messenger, coming out of the woodwork at odd hours of the night to whisper their desire for her over the dial-up internet. They told her that she was hot, that she could make her booty pop, that they wanted to see what else she could do. But the night that Jared, Max, and Charlie—a triumvirate of eighth graders—came over was the first time Elissa's efforts materialized.

"Who wants to get their ass kicked in air hockey?" Elissa asked the group from the privacy of my basement.

"You're on," Charlie replied, the least good-looking but most boisterous of the group.

It went on like this for a few hours. Us rotating turns on the air hockey table, an occasional game of foosball. For my fifth birthday, my grandfather had gifted me two vintage stuffed animal bears so large that their heads grazed the ceiling, with a girth so wide that not even the largest of the boys could fit his arms fully around them. At first Max and Charlie sat on the bears' laps, jokingly bouncing up and down in a bit of slapstick humor. But then all that bobbing grew into something greater, something more sexual. They flipped around and began to hump the bears in a wildly exaggerated fashion, laughing all the way.

"You guys are fucking ridiculous," Elissa told them.

"What are you guys even, like, doing?" I teased.

"You love it," said Max.

"You know it," Elissa said without skipping a beat.

Charlie and Max continued their thrusting as Elissa made her approach. Though it was Jared whom Elissa had made the plans with, he hung behind with me on the couch, opting out of all the revelry. Not because he wanted to hook up with me, but because he was actually attractive. Next to Charlie's and Max's ruddy complexions, Jared's taut and tanned form was striking. And when you're hot like that, you don't need to employ such theatrics. But it was precisely this type of display that Elissa was after. All the pomp and circumstance of Max and Charlie's perverted performance offered validation. She delighted in their willingness to humiliate themselves in the name of horniness, the fury of being wanted outweighing physical attraction ten to one.

"Let's go," she instructed Charlie and Max—and they obeyed.

The bathroom in my basement was down the corridor, past my mother's childhood jukebox, on the other side of the built-in bar. Elissa, who had been frequenting my home for nearly as long as me, served as their guide, leading them on the quick walk down the crunchy, colorless carpet. One turn to the left, another to the right, then straight into the bathroom, where they slammed the door shut. One small step for man, one giant, irrevocable leap for Elissa's reputation.

It all happened so fast. Jared and I: unmoving on the couch, unable to make the unnecessary small talk to mitigate our mutual unease. Elissa, Charlie, and Max: sandwiched in that slender, windowless bathroom, now made humid with desire. Despite my proximity, I never found out what truly happened in the bathroom. After all our endless machinations about kissing and cunnilingus, Elissa was shockingly proprietary when it came to the specifics of her first blow job. Or her first two, one completed right after the other, if the rumors were to be believed. The closest she came to divulging the details was the refrain she repeated as she jumped up and down on my twin-sized bed later that evening.

"I'm a slut now! I'm a slut now," she said over and over and over again.

"Sure are," I mustered, both jealous and judging.

Undeniably dazzled with herself, Elissa was high on her newly assured popularity. That night in my basement coincided with an oral sex panic that was spreading across the country. The *New York Times* had published an article claiming that middle schoolers were treating blow jobs like a goodnight kiss, the way they'd say goodbye after a date.[1] Paul Ruditis had recently released his 2005 novel *Rainbow Party*, a work of fiction that helped convince parents that kids were throwing parties where girls would wear different shades of lipstick to take turns sucking boys off, leaving a cacophony of colors across their cocks. Though I didn't know a soul who attended such a party, blow jobs did seem to be abundant. (Even among my friends, Elissa wasn't the only one giving them. She was just the loudest about it.) But in all the panic, parents were missing the point. There wasn't a newly heightened pressure from boys, or some latent response to Monica Lewinsky happening like they assumed. It was because some girls thought being a slut could make you a star.

In 2004, Paris Hilton's sex tape leaked. Come 2007, Kim

Kardashian's own video catapulted her to fame. In response, they owned their narratives, not so much reclaiming them as rebranding them as sexual empowerment. They posed for *Playboy* and palled around with the man behind *Girls Gone Wild*. Though these women weren't the true purveyors of the early aughts' raunch culture—it was Hugh Hefner who profited off their magazine spreads, Joe Francis who benefited from their proximity to the adult entertainment franchise—girls were responding to Paris and Kim. Like Nancy Jo Sales reported in a *New York* magazine cover story on New York City high schoolers in the late '90s, teens had started conceiving themselves in terms of "fame." She suggested that the "culture of celebrity" had become so omnipresent that it had "overtaken high school."[2]

While the media may have mocked Paris and Kim for only being famous because they had sex tapes, my friends and I started seeing sex as a shortcut to fame. If being known as a whore could allow Paris and Kim to dominate Hollywood, Elissa could only imagine how far being a "slut" would take her in Providence.

The plan worked, of course. Soon all of Providence seemed to know that Elissa was now *officially* a slut. Both because of Elissa's own efforts at dissemination and because I couldn't stop gossiping about it.

"Then she just literally brought them in there," I'd tell one friend.

"She's seriously such a whore," I texted another.

"I mean, she got what she wanted," I IM'd whoever would listen.

Despite it all I clung to Elissa. Still straddling the line between judgment and jealousy, I sought out my own form of rebellion. I wasn't courageous enough for the boys, so I delved into the booze. Seventh grade had ushered in bat mitzvah season, and we were busier than we'd ever been: spending every weekend attending at least one party, sometimes two. At my own bat mitzvah, my mom gave me a vodka cranberry to toast my newfound womanhood. I loved the drink, how cool I felt holding it, how simultaneously in control and out of control my brain seemed. And between my party and another of our temple classmate's, I realized these events were outfitted with more alcohol than the hosts could possibly track. So I devised a plan to swipe unattended drinks off the adults' table. Elissa and I set our sights on a white Russian, and when the retrieval proved successful, my role as the plan's mastermind gave me a greater rush than the swigs of the coffee liqueur. It gave me the feeling that I could be the catalyst of my life.

At the next bat mitzvah, I chugged a neglected rum and Coke alone. The following party, I replicated the experience with a margarita. Then I'd come into school the following Monday cosplaying a hungover Olsen twin: clutching a venti Starbucks beverage, wearing oversized beetle sunglasses. I'd feign headaches and discuss my fear that I needed to go to "AA." As Elissa continued to meet more boys, further solidifying her "slutty girl" status, drinking became the thing that made me *hard*. Elissa took to calling me her alchy; I alternated between lovingly referring to her as "skank" and "ho."

Because Elissa and I had gone to the same private school since nursery, the administrators were well aware of our dynamic. Throughout lower school they'd put Elissa and me in different classes to ensure we'd make other friends. Middle school was much the same. By the eighth grade they'd seen enough. Our principal, a small man with a soft cadence that Elissa frequently parodied, arranged appointments with both of us back to back. As I sat in his office for the first time, the meeting felt both surreal and inevitable.

"Do you know why you're here?" he asked me in his signature register.

"Because of my grades?" It was true, they had faltered. But we both knew I was skirting the truth.

"I think you have an image problem. If you keep this whole thing up, you're not going to last here through high school."

"I understand."

"Is there anything else you'd like to say?"

"Just that I, uh, really, really want to go to high school here."

"Then you're going to have to get it together."

Sitting there in his office is the first time I remember feeling deep, unrelenting shame. My parents had always treated me as an equal. I was more my mother's sister than her daughter. As much as I went to her for advice, she came to me for guidance, too. Talking to me openly about fights with my father, the relationship she'd found herself in with another mutual friend soon after. There were no rules in my house, no bedtimes or demands on my grades. In turn, there wasn't any disciplining. When I was caught drinking at a bat mitzvah and I tried to deny it, my father jokingly said to me, "Don't bullshit a bullshitter." Until that school meeting, nobody had ever spoken to me with such sternness. I felt humiliated, laid bare.

While I thought my meeting had gone poorly, Elissa was downright despondent. The principal had told her there was no longer a place for her at Wheeler. It was the first time Elissa had been led to believe that she was *bad*. A problem. Though it would be far from the last.

Feminist scholar Carol Gilligan argues that in adolescence, girls are encouraged to surrender their own perspectives. They're supposed to make themselves small, focus on becoming conventionally attractive and traditionally "nice," forgoing their confidence, spirit, and voice in favor of embodying these feminine mandates.[3] But Elissa was unwilling to do so, refusing to shrink herself down or deny her desires. In the eyes of many adults, she was becoming a rotten apple whose disobedience threatened to poison the greater well.

"Can you fucking believe this?" Elissa asked me.

"I mean, it's going to be okay. You'll just, like, go to PCD or something," I told her, referring to another one of Providence's less prestigious private schools. I assumed that though she'd no longer be at Wheeler, not much else in her life would change. That she'd stay, more or less, on track. I was wrong.

"That's easy for you to say, Sami."

"Seriously. Nobody's better at making friends than you."

Though I would have denied it, I secretly felt relieved that Elissa wasn't coming back. While so much of my friendship with Elissa was about having fun, being her friend wasn't always fun. A lot of my time was also spent consoling Elissa over the boys who would inevitably stop talking to her. Or supporting her when her slutty reputation would lead people to make up rumors about the extent of her sexual endeavors. Whom she'd slept with, and when. A lot of the time, it felt good to help Elissa. Talking her off the ledge felt like this special thing that only I could do, a gift I possessed. But deep down, I also knew I was talking out of my ass. Throwing words at the wall like spaghetti, hoping they'd stick. Worrying that I might slip up and say the wrong thing, no longer being the person who *got it*. Who got *her*.

CHAPTER V

Alyssa

In order for Alyssa's plan to work, an incredible constellation of coincidences had to coalesce in her favor. A lifetime's worth of good fortune cashed in, and then some. But in the end, all it really came down to was minutes. Forty-five of them, to be precise. Alyssa's flight from Hawaii to O'Hare International Airport was due to arrive in the afternoon. It had been three months since she'd been back in Northbrook, and this sojourn was just meant to be an ellipsis. A brief layover in the airport, where her mother would meet her and join her on yet another flight, to yet another program. Alyssa would only be in Illinois in theory, occupying a liminal space in practice.

O'Hare is the world's fourth-busiest airport. On any given day, more than nine hundred flights will depart from its runways. Like the ones I'd take after stopping there en route back to Southern California during my freshman year of college. I remember little of that year and even less of those trips, groggy from my grief. But on the day that Alyssa deplaned in Chicago, she was electrified with purpose. O'Hare and its 7,627 acres were no match for her.

"It's me," Alyssa said when she reached Morgan on a stranger's cell phone.

"What the fuck? Alyssa? How the fuck are you calling me right now?" Morgan asked.

"Listen, you gotta get here."

"Where? Where are you?"

"O'Hare."

"Shit. Okay."

When Alyssa's parents first approached her about attending Pacific Quest, she didn't put up much of a fight. Oftentimes parents will employ a transporter, someone who on average charges between $2,000 and $5,000 to wake their unsuspecting child up in the middle of the night and accompany them to their designated troubled teen program, against their will. Depending on the teenager's degree of defiance, varying levels of aggression are employed. Some have had their hands tied, others handcuffed. Parents enter a contract with the transporters to make these measures possible. The affidavit they sign transfers temporary parental rights to them, giving them the power to authorize medical attention, restrain the teen, or anything else they see fit. Whatever it takes to get the child to the program, by any means necessary.

Elissa's own mother had hired a transporter, having them take Elissa from her bedroom and bring her to a wilderness program in Montana. But Alyssa was compliant. She left for Hawaii without an escort; they planned for her to return unchaperoned as well.

Louise and Richard trusted her, and in truth, they were also exasperated by the expense of a transporter. The price of Pacific Quest itself was already breathtaking. They couldn't fathom tacking so many more thousands onto the bill.

Located on the Big Island, Pacific Quest rests on the Hilo Bay coastline where the waves appear indigo, becoming cerulean closer to the shore. Its beauty belies its truth: The bay is referred to as the "tsunami capital of the United States." The surf there is so severe that locals discourage even the strongest of swimmers from taking a dip. Along with its bay views, Pacific Quest's campus, which is still open to this day, also houses freshwater ponds, botanical gardens, and banana trees aplenty. These were the spoils of nature that sold Louise, along with the more tenable living conditions, the participants sleeping inside instead of outdoors, a practice common in other wilderness programs.

The sprawling sanctuary-like environment depicted in the promotional materials Louise reviewed wasn't exaggerated. But nearly a quarter of Alyssa's days were spent not in its splendor, but rather within the confines of her *hale*. Pacific Quest likes to incorporate localisms into their vernacular, *hale* meaning "house" in Hawaiian. This particular home is a human-sized chicken coop consisting of three walls; a squat space fitting a plastic folding chair, yoga mat, and bin of belongings. One that faces decidedly away from the ocean.

Pacific Quest is divided into different camps that participants graduate through. The first "camp" at Pacific Quest is Nalu, which takes its title from the Hawaiian word for *reflect*. In it, activities taking place outside of the hale are more sparse. A composition notebook and a pamphlet of yoga poses are the primary sources of entertainment. But come Ohana—which means "family," the third camp—days are spent gardening, weeding invasive species, and tending to the banana trees.

Community is also encouraged in Ohana, and it was then that Alyssa met her fellow campers. There were Lauren and Allie, the "normal" girls who had come from suburban backgrounds similar to Alyssa's. The boys, like Ryan and Alex, who lusted after her, despite the uniform of maroon cotton shorts, waterproof Keens, and sun hats she was given to wear. Then there were the kids who wore their damage on their sleeves: the thirteen-year-old boy with oppositional defiant disorder, the girl experiencing heroin withdrawal, another with an eating disorder who was frequently reprimanded for hiding her food.

Alyssa grew closest to Lauren, who tells me about her time at Pacific Quest with both skepticism and reverence. Lauren had chosen to go to Pacific Quest and feels that she benefited from her time there. She became a better-mannered, more obedient teenager. But she still managed to have some moments of misbehavior. Like when she and Alyssa were issued "earshots," what Pacific Quest calls the punishment for talking without a counselor nearby. But nothing would stop Alyssa from gossiping about boys. She and Allie both had a crush on one of the counselors—an entirely average-looking twenty-something with a buzz cut, benefiting greatly from their wilderness goggles—yet mostly Alyssa longed to be back home with Owen. When Alyssa received a letter from Owen that detailed just how much he missed her, too, Lauren recalls the effect it had on Alyssa as unmistakable. Each molecule of her being, newly recharged. So much so that Alyssa even started talking about Owen in group therapy.

"He's just the best," Alyssa said when it was her time to speak.

"I mean, he does heroin sometimes. But that's not *who* he is.

"Regardless, I don't care. I love him no matter what."

It felt good to talk about Owen out loud, to declare him hers to a full group, not just in her quiet out-of-earshot whispers with Lauren. So good, in fact, that it blinded her to the extent of what was happening behind the scenes. That her counselors were relaying this information to her parents, harnessing it as a tool to convince them to keep her in the Troubled Teen Industry much longer than they'd anticipated.

Like Alyssa, teens are often introduced to the industry through a short-term wilderness program. While the teens are there, the staff will likely prey on the parents as much as the students. Typically they'll start by suggesting to the parents that they have their child stay on for another few weeks, which can turn into a few months, and so on. Eventually, the program might propose that their teen be transitioned to a therapeutic boarding school, a recommendation that persuades 40 to 45 percent of parents to send their child to places like Ponca Pines directly from the wilderness progam. It's part of the process of easing a parent into the industry: having them agree to this initial short-term separation, in preparation for later selling them on a long-term stay at a boarding school. All of which contributes to the $1.2 billion profit the industry turns annually, both from the kickbacks the wilderness programs make from referring teens to boarding school, and from the exorbitant tuition rates that meet parents upon their child's arrival.

Shortly after Owen's letter arrived, Alyssa learned that her parents would be sending her to Carlbrook, a therapeutic boarding school in rural southern Virginia. Alyssa didn't take well to this news, seeming to realize for the first time that she'd been deemed so "troubled" that she had to be isolated from Northbrook, her friends, and Owen even longer than she'd anticipated. *This is bullshit*, she thought only to herself. Until the afternoon she and Lauren found themselves playing with the stray feral cats that often found their way onto the campus. Pawing through the cats' ungroomed, flee-ridden fur, Alyssa vocalized the reservations she'd been having about Carlbrook—along with the alternative she'd been scheming.

"What if I ran away?"

———

Tyler's car was his prized possession. A crimson fortieth-anniversary Mustang V6 finished with cream racing stripes. A two-door with the kind of cramped back seat that made pretzels out of its passengers' limbs, unappealing enough to provoke a war over who rode shotgun. But on the day that Alyssa arrived at O'Hare, Tyler, Morgan, and Owen didn't have time to contemplate the seating chart. The details Alyssa had provided Morgan were sparse—and the window of time within which they had to extract her was exceedingly slender—but they were just high enough on adrenaline and teenage aplomb.

"Holy shit, I think that's her," Morgan said.

"Where?" Owen asked.

"There! Holy shit, she looks just like she did in the pictures."

She'd taken to stalking Pacific Quest's website, showing the boys the various photos the Pacific Quest staff had posted of Alyssa picking pineapples. An option I didn't know I had when Elissa was sent away. Instead, I was left to imagine where Elissa was. Daydreaming about who she was with and what she was doing. Wondering if she was having fun, if she even missed her old life at all.

"Alyssa!!!"

"Aaaaaaaalyssaaaaaa!!!"

In the years that followed, Tyler, Morgan, Owen, and Alyssa took to calling the day at O'Hare "the kidnapping." The title had a better ring to it than "the runaway"—cheekier, more dramatic—even though the latter bore more truth. It's not like Owen had taken Alyssa against her will. Breaking out was a choice she'd initiated, a plan she'd conceived. One they all ultimately delighted in, later describing the experience as if they'd robbed a bank. Tyler, commanding the getaway car. Alyssa, sprinting as she leaped into the vehicle, right into Owen's arms. A salacious story that skirted the fact that as they made their escape, Alyssa's mother was waiting for her in the airport. "I'll never forget the horrible feeling of running desperately around O'Hare trying to find her," Louise writes, tormented by it even now.

Back at Owen's, Alyssa knew she was living on borrowed time. They hadn't driven to Canada; she hadn't even left the county. Alyssa called her older brother, and while she neglected to tell him her whereabouts, she promised him that she was safe and just needed some time away. Still, the fleeting nature of her and

Owen's reunion only added to the romanticism of it all. Each kiss could potentially be the last, every bong hit, the final one. They buried themselves away in that room of his above the garage—a basement by another name, a den of debauchery in the sky rather than underground—getting drunk and trading declarations of love.

"You'll wait for me, right?" Alyssa asked Owen as they sprawled out on the futon, one of the space's lone pieces of furniture.

"I'd wait for you for...forever," he said.

"But what about other girls?"

"You think I give a fuck about other girls? The fuck?"

"No, but..."

"I could ask you the same thing about other dudes."

"You're the literal love of my life."

"Me too, baby. Me too."

Back at Wheeler, my friends and I talked about love in terms of our senses. The boys we liked smelled good to us; the aroma of love offered yet another piece of evidence that we were bound to one another. There's a fine line between quintessential teenage obsession—an all-consuming, drama-prone type of romance— and true emotional dependence. What Alyssa and Owen shared was the troubling kind, rooted in her depression and their love of drugs. A much more problematic foundation for a relationship than just hyperbolic, hormone-driven emotions.

The kidnapping ultimately only lasted three days. Eventually, Alyssa returned home, ready to accept her fate. But those seventy-two hours provided enough time for Alyssa's parents to rightfully feel afraid about Alyssa's well-being anew. But for Alyssa, it was a long enough stretch of time for her love to teeter over the edge from a high school infatuation into a low-functioning emotional dependence. A dependence that is inextricable from her demise.

Young women are raised on stories like this: the prince, the white knight, the soul mate. The perils of these tropes are something Nina Renata Aron writes about in the 2020 *Good Morning, Destroyer of Men's Souls: A Memoir of Women, Addiction, and Love*, her account of being in a relationship with an addict. Reflecting on how codependency looks a lot like the versions of "true love" we see in books, film, and television. That given our society's perpetuation of these models, the line between healthy and toxic love can be difficult to discern, sometimes even appearing aspirational instead of worrisome.

Outside of wanting to emulate *Wuthering Heights'* Heathcliff and Catherine and have someone love you so much they'd dig your corpse out of a grave, if you're struggling like Alyssa, awash in anxiety and depression, losing your sense of autonomy is alluring. Having someone to take refuge in, an external force to take the pain away. But this dynamic also halted Alyssa's development, hindering her from figuring out how to self-soothe or problem solve on her own. Something she'd continue to struggle with, long after breaking up with Owen.

CHAPTER VI

Alissa

Alissa came of age in her basement, too. Graduating from taking her first real swigs of alcohol within its wood-paneled walls to barricading herself down there, partying with the zeal of someone who was no longer a novice. By junior year, Alissa had grown even closer to Lily, who often bunked down there with her. Alissa's mom was still gone most evenings, and Lily was there night after night on the couch with her boyfriend. Both girls reveled in their freedom. But Lily knew her limits, while Alissa always had another blunt to be smoked, an additional bottle to be drunk, one more boy to invite over. In the absence of any other supervision, Alissa and Lily's relationship took on a familiar dynamic. Parallel to Elissa and me, Lily became Alissa's caretaker. Serving as her designated driver, a voice of reason, the person constantly trying to persuade her to *chill the fuck out*.

Speaking to Lily reminds me of the times I tried to reason with Elissa. Too timid in my disposition, too complacent in our dynamic to do much more than subtly urge her to reconsider her choices. Though Lily was much more forceful—able to tell Alissa exactly what she was feeling—her warnings also often fell on deaf ears. Frustrating Lily in a way that's still apparent as she tells me about a night the two spent driving around West Omaha in Lily's Hyundai Tiburon.

Alissa and Lily were going to the Ozarks the following morning, and Lily had convinced Alissa to not drink for the night in anticipation of all the partying that awaited them. There was a harmony between them that evening until Lily clocked Alissa discreetly taking pulls from a bottle. Enraged, Lily pulled over in a nearby parking lot to physically remove the bottle from Alissa's hands. She was mad at Alissa for going back on her word, and even angrier that she was stuck being the buzzkill. Alissa retaliated with force, lunging over the center console, igniting a flurry of poorly landed punches, scratches, and slaps between the girls— until Lily's teeth connected with the thin stretch of skin beneath Alissa's eye. With the shock of Alissa's blood in her mouth, Lily paused, and Alissa did as well. The two of them sitting there, laughing and laughing, both having surrendered.

Many of their nights played out like this. Lily, driving them around as they bumped Lil Wayne and Kid Cudi on her car speakers, waiting to see where the night took them. Alissa, riding shotgun, laser-focused on procuring a means of inebriation.

"I'm gonna grab some Swishers. Want anything?" Alissa asked one evening after they'd pulled over at a Kum & Go so Lily could refill her tank.

"Nah, I'm good," Lily said.

"Be right back."

"Word."

Though Lily neglected to go inside with Alissa, she was able to observe enough from her car window to realize the same scene she'd seen play out many times before was about to take the stage.

Entering the convenience store, Alissa walked up to the front where they kept the Swisher Sweets cigarillos, her favorite for rolling blunts in all the white grape, strawberry, or tropical fusion flavors. She pocketed a pack and then kept making her way along the refrigerators lined with Dr Peppers, Monster Energy drinks, and VitaminWater Zero Sugars until she was in the liquor section. This wasn't Alissa's first rodeo—her guy friends had started stealing booze from the Kum & Go and she quickly followed suit. She'd take her time with it, pore over the fare before going in for the kill. It was the same strategy I employed the first time I shoplifted. Elissa and I were in eighth grade and meeting up with a new friend of hers, Brynn, at a candy store after school. Jealous of the attention Elissa had started paying her, I lifted a packet of Razzles to impress them. Trying my hardest to act nonchalant in the lead-up, much like Alissa did as she scanned the aisles of the convenience store.

"Anything I can help you with?" the cashier called from the front of the store.

"All good, all good," Alissa replied.

"Just shout if you need anything."

"Cool."

There are Kum & Gos scattered throughout Nebraska, and Alissa had frequented them for as long as she could remember.

Each being indistinguishable from another, painted over in the chain's signature fire engine red and illuminated in industrial fluorescent lighting. The same incandescence Alissa was basking in as she started pulling handles off the shelf, dropping them into her bag too hastily to stop the harsh clanking that comes when a bottle hits a bottle.

"Hey, what do you think you're doing?" The clanking had tipped off the clerk, who beelined his way to the back of the store.

"Nothing, dude."

"There's cameras in here. I know what you're doing!"

"Back the fuck off!"

As a child Alissa would shut down when she didn't get her way, pleading at her parents until they gave in. This taught her that getting what you wanted was always an option; you just had to fight for it. And when the clerk attempted to pry the bottles out of Alissa's hand, the same fury that overcame her in the car with Lily took hold of her. She started swinging at him. "What the fuck are you doing?" she yelled. "Give it back!"

"You're psycho. I'm calling the cops."

"Don't you fucking dare."

"Watch me."

The clerk made his way to the front of the store, where he phoned 911. Alissa hadn't worried about the consequences of her actions. Pop culture taught us that when white, privileged women do get in trouble, they typically just get slaps on the wrist. When Lindsay Lohan was arrested, she spent eighty-four minutes in jail. Nicole Richie's stay was even shorter, eighty-two minutes behind bars. Their arrests were treated as punch lines and tabloid fodder.

Much like having a crotch shot or a sex tape, getting in trouble with the law was just another opportunity for Perez Hilton to plaster a celebrity's mugshot across his site. They were not treated as crimes, just content for me and the rest of the public to devour and then discard—nothing more, nothing less.

When I myself shoplifted the Razzles, I didn't consider the potential damage to my future. I just considered myself to be like Winona Ryder shoplifting from Saks. Her wily eyes, her famously slight frame hidden beneath a trench. What I didn't realize was that what actually united Winona and me was that we could afford to pay bail, hire a lawyer. She, Alissa, and I all had a privilege that made us relatively immune to the more severe consequences of the criminal justice system. We were safe to break bad as we pleased.

While the clerk was on the line with the police, Alissa made a run for it. Sprinting past the Hostess snacks display stand, moving faster by the gas pumps. Lily watched the fight play out from her car window, driving off when things started to look dicey. Alissa took to cornfields across the street, splaying down in the dirt, attempting to camouflage herself beneath the stalks.

"Jesus," Claire said as she entered the station to get her daughter.

The cops apprehended Alissa in the cornfield, bringing her down to the precinct. This wasn't the first time Claire had been down this road with one of her kids. Her older son, Matt, was frequently in trouble with the law. But his indiscretions far exceeded the limits of bad teenage behavior. "Swatting" first made head-lines in 2008, when people on the dark web began calling the police with fictional emergencies. Bomb threats, hostage situa-tions, murder. While this may sound like a heightened form of prank phone calling, it's a much more acute form of harassment. These calls trigger a SWAT team to descend on whatever address is shared, often the home of one of the caller's enemies. People have died and others have been seriously injured as a result, lead-ing legislators to push to classify the act as terrorism. And this was the world Matt had become enmeshed in—resulting in a litany of investigations, charges, and later on, arrests. When Claire walked into the station, she kept thinking about not being ready to go through something like this again.

"Mom, I'm—" Alissa said.

"Save it," Claire said.

"You don't understand, I was just getting snacks and—"

"Trust me, I understand."

Claire was enraged, but taking in the totality of the situation, her anger turned to anguish. Realizing that the problem wasn't Alissa's actions themselves, but the root of them. That she was so desperate for alcohol that she was willing to steal it, so eager to party that she would do whatever it took. It wasn't about *what* Alissa had done, but *why* she did it.

"Seriously, Mom."

"Let's just talk about this at home."

"Fine."

"Good."

After the arrest, Alissa was forced to appear in court, and later pay a fine. A meager punishment, but one that went on her permanent record. Creating physical, concrete proof that she was trouble. And soon after, Claire started to look for help. This is how the Troubled Teen Industry typically recruits families. A harmless, cursory Google search will spin into inquiries on a website for various facets of the industry. An educational consultant, who masquerades as a college counselor type, is often essential to the equation. They guide parents—like Alyssa's and Elissa's, who both employed them—through finding the best wilderness program, then therapeutic boarding school, for their child. What parents often don't realize is that the consultants are often receiving financial kickbacks from these programs, earning a fee each time they place someone in their care.

Claire didn't employ a consultant, having found Ponca Pines on her own. And for the first time in a long time, Claire felt hopeful. Yet there was still an obstacle in her way: John. Claire had married John when she was just nineteen years old. They grew up together: becoming parents, then homeowners, maturing during their partnership. Even though he'd broken her heart, she still needed his buy-in as a coparent. All matters pertaining to Alissa were difficult for them to discuss. John was upset that Alissa refused to visit him. The idea of boarding school didn't sit well with him, either.

"What is boarding school going to solve?" John asked.

"John, you're not with her every day. You're not seeing it," Claire said.

"Because she won't come here. It's not like I don't *want* to see her."

"I know, I know. That's not what I'm trying to say. I'm just really worried."

The Troubled Teen Industry plays on parents' vulnerability. Claire was at the end of her rope: so worried about Alissa's future and well-being that she was desperate for some relief, any solution. According to many parents who have sent their teens to these programs, the educational consultants and program directors appear hyperaware of their concerns. The Alliance for the Safe, Therapeutic and Appropriate Use of Residential Treatment (A START) reported that recruiters typically stick to a script similar to this: "You've called just in time. We've seen this before. You need to enroll your child without delay. If you don't, your child is on a path to jail, a mental hospital, the gutter, or the morgue. It sounds like you've lost control as a parent, and the only way to get control back is to let us impose discipline in a controlled environment. Let me take your application—right now. Remember, your child is in danger and there is no time to lose."

"I'm sending her no matter what."

"We'll see about that."

Claire's desperation to send Alissa to Ponca Pines now makes sense to me. Why she and so many other parents would find it nearly impossible not to succumb to what these programs offer. I believe it's because of the industry's assurance that they'll save their children from harm as well as rehabilitate them without any greater, societal consequences. Because they're boarding schools, not actual rehabs. And as such, a child's attendance is only a slight deviation from their preordained path, not a true pivot. These schools appear to offer a safety net, keeping upper-class teens on the right trajectory to college, careers, prosperity.

That promise was all Claire knew of the Troubled Teen

Industry; the press surrounding it was primarily positive. Though some exposés were written—including Maia Szalavitz's seminal 2006 exploration of the industry, *Help at Any Cost: How the Troubled-Teen Industry Cons Parents and Hurts Kids*—the reigning narrative was that these institutions that practiced "tough love" were still the most viable solution for curbing a teen's behavior. With articles detailing how Roseanne Barr, Barbara Walters, Kathy Hilton, and Farrah Fawcett had sent their kids to similar programs. Or that Nancy Reagan, George H. W. Bush, and Princess Diana had all visited Straight, Incorporated: a chain of teen residential rehabilitation centers.

It wasn't until 2020—when Paris Hilton released her documentary, *This Is Paris*—that the floodgates opened for conversations surrounding the dangers of the Troubled Teen Industry to hit the mainstream.

By 2020, my fascination with Paris had waned, yet I still found myself floored and stunned as Paris revealed that she'd attended Provo Canyon School, a therapeutic boarding school that's still open to this day in Utah, where she alleges that she was restrained, involuntarily medicated, and placed in solitary confinement. Later she'd state that she was sexually assaulted by a non-medically-certified staff member, who digitally penetrated her while claiming to be performing a cervical exam late one evening.

Taking in the news, I was overcome by a familiar yet unnerving sensation. A desire to call Elissa. To let her know that Paris had also been sent away. That our idol had shared this experience as well.

In the weeks that followed the film's release, an entire generation of former Troubled Teen Industry students began coming forward on TikTok. They shared their own stories of abuse, neglect, and trauma. The hashtag #TroubledTeenIndustry has since garnered over 337 million views. But, as I'd later learn, these conversations weren't just happening on TikTok. I also found that some of Elissa's former classmates had started to identify as survivors rather than graduates. They maintained this heightened sense of urgency when we eventually spoke—wanting the truth of their experience to be known, too.

CHAPTER VII

Elissa

While I was in high school, people in Providence kept disappearing: my friend Ruby's brother, Frank; Julia's older brother, James; various kids who went to Providence's other private schools. Without any formal announcement as to where they went, students were left to sift through the rumors. All we knew for sure was that Ruby's brother had looted his school's locker room, pocketing cell phones and iPods. Though he was never charged with a crime, one day his parents sent him away to a school for "troubled teens." Julia's brother also had a similar story. He was drinking too much and getting suspended nearly as often. Then he was gone. Off to another troubled teen school.

Leaving day school for a boarding school after ninth grade was a common occurrence in Providence. We applauded our classmates who went on to New England's storied institutions, like Choate, Deerfield, or Andover, believing that they'd have a better shot at the Ivy League colleges. But the kinds of boarding schools that Julia's and Ruby's siblings went to were something else entirely. Few knew their names or where exactly they were located. Unlike our friends who decamped to the Exeters of the world, there was no coming home for Thanksgiving or summer vacation. Once they were gone, they stayed gone.

Some fifty thousand teens will get sent to these types of troubled teen programs per year, many coming from suburbs like my own.[1] But we didn't do too much probing into their vanishings. My friends' siblings' exile seemed strange, not uncommon. When students would actually get up the nerve to ask their parents how their kids were doing, we'd get their well-crafted responses, like, *Frank's really taking to the new environment* or *James is getting to do so many extracurriculars.* To push any further would be impolite, a breach in the mutually agreed upon suburban social contract to keep any questions or conversation about these vanishings light. As a result, our questions about their whereabouts and well-being went unanswered.

Elissa was in her sophomore year at St. Andrew's when she became the next person to disappear. We were less in touch by then. My principal had made good on his word, allowing me to stay at Wheeler for high school. So I attempted to make good on my word, too. Trading in my Ugg boots and Juicy sweats for BDG skinny jeans, faux-vintage band T-shirts, and Dr. Martens. Reading books like *The Fountainhead*, *On the Road*, and *Less than Zero*. Applying for Wheeler's literary magazine and newspaper. Forging ahead, reborn: a "hipster."

Still, when the news reached me that Elissa had been transferred from St. Andrew's to an unknown troubled teen school, it was a shock to my system. I no longer cared about social niceties. I plied everyone for every bit of information I could gather about Elissa. Rebecca, who was still dating my father. Faye, Rebecca's daughter and Elissa's favorite cousin. Pestering them incessantly for any last detail. Not stopping to think that if I was missing Elissa, my pain paled in comparison to what her family was feeling. The agony her mother, siblings, and cousins were experiencing in her absence.

Though I didn't learn much about Spring Ridge Academy back then, I've more than made up for lost time. Breaking Code Silence was founded in 2021 and is the preeminent nonprofit fighting for the rights of Troubled Teen Industry survivors and for institutional reform, and was featured heavily in *This Is Paris*. In the wake of the doc, I've taken to talking to the staff regularly. Coming to them with questions about the industry's origins, the policies that enable it to stay in place, the strange behavioral exercises that crop up time and time again in my conversations with former students. More often than not, it's Lex who takes my calls: a young trans man with a soft smile and a trio of nose piercings. Lex went to SRA and has an encyclopedic knowledge of the school, which is still in operation. Patiently walking me through SRA's history, beginning with its founding in 1997 as a private, parent-choice secondary school for teenage girls grappling with everything from eating disorders to drug use to defiance.

Until 2016, the school was run by Ruth, a middle-aged woman with charcoal eyes. Early on, she operated it out of a meager house with an attached barn, only being able to accommodate a handful of girls at a time. But in the intervening years, they were able to build out the campus. Its aesthetic came to embrace the school's desert environment, with stucco buildings and sand-colored pathways. By the time Elissa enrolled in the school they were able to house upward of fifty students at a time, offering them state-of-the-art facilities like sand volleyball courts, science labs, and an ornate seating area boasting a fountain topped with a Romanesque statue of a woman.

As Lex frequently underscores on our calls, there is no federal oversight or government-sanctioned standards when it comes to the Troubled Teen Industry. Therapeutic boarding schools are independently operated, so Ruth has been able to run it as she sees fit, bringing in her son and daughter-in-law—neither of whom has a degree in psychology, as there's no governing body mandating that practitioners have the proper credentials—to serve as her deputies.

A common practice in the Troubled Teen Industry is the use of operant conditioning, a method created by American psychologist B. F. Skinner in late 1940 in which "good" behavior is reinforced with rewards so it will be repeated, and "bad" behavior is punished in order to eliminate it. Though Spring Ridge denies the use of operant conditioning, many of the school's rules and regulations seem to enforce the practice. Spring Ridge makes students follow a rigid schedule of therapy, exercise, and schooling. They also implement a strict style code, allowing the girls to use only light pink nail polish and banning the boys from using Old Spice or any products considered too "masculine." Follow along and the school will grant you privileges: more access to phone calls, visits home, and ultimately, the right to graduate. If not, your privileges will be stripped from you. Everything from the right to call home to the right to speak to classmates or even have privacy. In the most severe cases of disobedience, a staffer will even watch as you sleep, use the bathroom, and shower.

Rule following never came easily to Elissa. She didn't like that they often had to wake up at six a.m. to work out. She wasn't athletic and had no interest in being so. In eighth grade we tried out for soccer together, only to both be placed on the sixth-grade team. At Spring Ridge, Elissa dreaded how all seventy-five-odd girls would gather on the athletic field, fashioning their yoga mats for group stretches in a haphazard circle before running for twenty minutes around the field.

The girls staggered around, jogging in clusters. Elissa kept to the middle, where the largest mass of them hovered, attempting to blend in enough to power walk. A laziness that almost always went noticed, incensing the staff.

"Look alive out there, Elissa."

"I mean it. Faster, Elissa!"

After morning exercises, the girls usually retired to their rooms for chores, alternating between making their beds, doing laundry, and tidying up the dorm. Elissa lived with Mackenzie and Abby and the three had grown close, also buddying up to Hannah, who lived down the hall. Hannah had been at Spring Ridge longer than the others and had earned the right to go on long weekend visits to her family in New York. Upon her return, she'd dole out stories to her roommates about how she'd hooked up with an ex, or that she'd snuck out of her parents' apartment. She had to trust the girls not to tattle to the administration—snitching on your classmates to gain more privileges was a common practice at therapeutic boarding schools.

"So I saw Michael," Hannah said after checking to make sure the roaming staffers who monitored the dorm hallways and eavesdropped on their conversations were out of earshot.

"Oh my god, tell us everything," Abby said. She was younger than the others, sent away before losing her virginity, and eager to live through the romantic experiences of her friends. Elissa would later teach her how to masturbate with the school-sanctioned electric toothbrushes.

"Okay, so we were fully hooking up," Hannah said.

"Like sex? Or did you give him head?" Elissa said, showing off her sexual knowledge.

"He was fingering me, but, like, really fingering me."

"Did you cum?"

"Oh yeah. I definitely did."

"Slut."

They'd go on like this, Hannah offering sojourns into the outside world; Elissa sharing the exploits of her prior sex life. Soon it wasn't enough to remember the tingle of being touched. They wanted to experience the thrills in real time.

At Spring Ridge, it was hard to get your hands on anything. Sharpies were monitored in case of huffing. Girls shaved with electric razors because Gillettes and their ilk were restricted in case of attempts to slit their wrists. But one of Elissa's roommates, who asked not to be identified, managed to sneak in a single razor blade. She suddenly tenses up when we speak about the cutting, as if she still fears retribution from SRA, or as if she still hasn't shed the paranoia that comes from having spent so much of her life under such heavy surveillance. She becomes more reticent and reserved as she talks about hiding the razor in the binding of the library's sole copy of *Hamlet*.

One in four American teen girls will, at some point, harm herself without any suicidal intentions.[2] While boys are more likely to hit themselves, cutting is more frequently young women's method of self-harm. Research from the American Psychological Association explains that teens self-harm because it helps them move from feeling agitated to feeling calm.[3] Or because it can be a way to prompt attention or sympathy. But the reason that confounds and captivates me the most is that self-harm can be a way to achieve an altered state of being, prompting a sensation so vast it washes away all else that preceded it.

Elissa had experienced the sensation before. She'd started cutting in the eighth grade, not long after a few of our friends had admitted to dabbling in it. At lunch she'd pull me into the bathroom stall at school, showing me some of her first attempts. In the beginning, the lines looked more like scratches than true cuts. Surface level enough that they reminded me of the burns we'd make on our hands by pouring salt on them and then placing ice on the mound, seeing who could withstand the most pain. All I could think was that the cuts were just another method by which Elissa was seeking attention; I feigned interest in them before changing the topic of conversation.

A few months after Elissa started cutting, she called me from her bathroom at home. I'd get late-night calls from her often—her crying over a fight she'd had with her mom, some boy, another friend—but this time there was a deeper, more disturbing panic in her voice. The blade had gone too deep, puncturing far too much of her wrist.

"Shit, Sami, shit," Elissa said.

"Do you think you need stitches?" I asked.

"I'm not getting fucking stitches."

"Should we call your mom?"

"If you tell anyone I'll kill you. Seriously."

I stayed on the phone with Elissa until the bleeding subsided, and then lay awake for many hours afterward. The blood had been so visceral to me that I felt as if I could taste its iron on my tongue. By midnight I couldn't hold it in any longer. I woke up my mother, tears pouring so rapidly down my face that they actually turned my saliva viscous with their salt. In the morning my mom called the school nurse, and they alerted Elissa's mother. When Elissa got called into the health center, she knew there was only one person to blame.

"I can't believe you."

"I'm sorry."

"I could care less what you have to say."

She didn't speak to me for the next three days. Smirking at me from across the gymnasium in phys ed. Shit talking me to our other friends. The anxiety her actions provoked felt so all-encompassing, it grew physical. Over the course of that week, I experienced debilitating stomach pain every morning before school. When she glanced in my direction, I felt flashes of vertigo. Later on, after we'd reconciled, I saw the wound up close. How quickly it had healed in such a short period of time made me realize that Elissa had exaggerated the amount of blood. *Fucking attention-seeking bitch*, I thought to myself.

For Mackenzie, Hannah, Abby, and Elissa, cutting was an act of loyalty. If they all self-harmed, none of them could rat the others out without getting in trouble, too. So each girl took a turn checking the copy of *Hamlet* out from the library, taking their turn with the razor blade before returning the book, then off to the next.

"Hey, girl, where's that copy of *Hamlet*?" Elissa asked Rose, a student who volunteered as the school's librarian, upon entering the library.

"Your turn to recite the monologue?" Rose asked, referring to one of their English class assignments.

"Oh yeah."

"It's back with the *S*'s, let me know if you can't find it."

"Thanks, girl!"

Back in her dorm room, Elissa flipped through the pages until she came across the contraband. Hiding in the bathroom as she took the blade to her flesh, tracing shallow parallel lines against her translucent skin, she felt more like herself than she had since she'd arrived on Spring Ridge's campus. She hadn't stopped cutting after her mother found out. Elissa had only started slicing up her inner thighs instead of her wrists.

Cutting was an act I couldn't intellectualize, one that seemed vulgar to me. Until I came across Leslie Jamison's 2014 essay "The Grand Unified Theory of Female Pain" and the desire finally crystallized for me: "People say cutters are just doing it for the attention, but what's that 'just' about? A cry for attention is positioned as a crime, as if attention were inherently a selfish thing to want. But isn't wanting attention one of the most fundamental traits of being human—and isn't granting it one of the most important gifts we can ever give?"

Cutting had become the way that Hannah, Abby, Mackenzie, and Elissa sought and received attention from one another. The gift they gave each other, both in loyalty and in feeling seen. And though Ruth didn't know about the cutting, she did notice a shift in Elissa's behavior. Teachers were complaining about that smirk of hers, how she'd deploy it when they called on her in class. There were reports of her yelling out nonsensical phrases like *fry my fallopian tubes on a barbecue* to make the other girls laugh. She'd refuse to say anything more than a few words in therapy. While Ruth typically ruled with a quiet malevolence—known for maintaining an unflappable demeanor—Elissa's behavior seemed to enrage her, leading her to action.

A long-held practice in the Troubled Teen Industry is the use of attack therapy, a confrontational exercise in which a therapist or other participants heavily criticize students. Synanon, the 1958 rehab turned cult from which TTI programs sprang, popularized the practice. Founded by Chuck Dederich, Synanon intended to build on the principles of Alcoholics Anonymous to help those grappling with drug addiction. But as Synanon evolved, it became more and more reliant on what they called "The Game," a form of attack therapy during which members were made to endure intense and profanity-laced criticism from their peers, often leading to both physical and verbal abuse.

Synanon devolved in the late 1970s—after they were discovered to have committed more than eighty violent acts, including the mass beatings of teenagers, who were hospitalized from the assaults—but not before its gospel spread. In 1967, former Synanon member Mel Wasserman founded CEDU, the first-ever therapeutic boarding school, molded in Synanon's image, from the use of attack therapy to Dederich's withholding of members' rights.

While Spring Ridge denies any use of attack therapy, the school does practice "feedback groups." These groups operate in much the same way as traditional attack therapy, even though, in the years since Synanon and CEDU, research has shown these practices can lead to lasting psychological harm. Still, they'd gather students in a circle, placing one of them in what the students referred to as the "hot seat." Facilitators then encouraged the other participants to offer feedback to whoever was in the hot seat. With the girls hurling "constructive criticism" at them while the one in the hot seat had to sit there and take it, without any room for rebuttal.

If a student couldn't be motivated by rewards, the hot seat was the alternative. Where students would have their secrets exposed, their flaws broadcasted, and their biggest insecurities brought to the surface. To me, it was an example of punishment by way of shaming. A way to amplify the inner voice within each girl that whispers they're *grotesque, distasteful, wrong.* The same tool employed by religion, society, and the government to keep women down, now deployed by the Troubled Teen Industry to compel students to change their bad behavior.

At Spring Ridge, Elissa frequently found herself in the hot seat. Going round after round, week after week. Being endlessly reminded of just how ashamed of herself she should be.

"Who has something to say to Elissa?" Ruth asked during one feedback group. She didn't usually run the feedback groups, leaving that to her deputies, but Elissa was a case that required a heavy hitter.

"C'mon, one of you must have something to say to Elissa."

"She does the best eyebrows," one girl said. Elissa was the go-to eyebrow tweezer on campus.

"We both know you can do better than that."

"I think she's a taker," the girl said. According to a former Spring Ridge philosophy, the world is divided between those who give and those who take—and to be a taker is to place yourself on the wrong side of the divide.

"Now we're getting somewhere. Anyone else?"

"She just . . . sits there."

"How does that make you feel?"

"Like she's so annoying."

"Like I wanna slap that stupid smirk off her face."

"Elissa, how does that make you feel?" Ruth asked.

"Elissa?"

"Got it," Elissa said.

"Seriously? What is your problem? Can you just say something? Anything?" Ruth said in an octave that was much deeper, more irate than her regular pitch.

None of the girls had ever heard Ruth speak like that before. Self-possession was her superpower. But Elissa's behavior was like a cockroach in Ruth's school—no matter the condemnation, it was near impossible to kill it.

In the end, it was Ruth who surrendered. She recommended that Elissa move on from Spring Ridge. Elissa's mother, who knew how difficult her daughter could be in the face of authority, didn't think to doubt Ruth's assessment. Especially given the fact that she wasn't allowed to hear Elissa's side. Communication is often restricted at therapeutic boarding schools. In some, there may be a staffer listening in on the line. When students write letters home, the staff often reads them ahead of time, sometimes crossing out any salacious lines or throwing them away altogether. And if a student is somehow able to get through to their parents the truth of their experience, the staff might play their trump card: reminding families that this is the kind of lying and manipulation they sent their kids away for in the first place. Who were they to be trusted?

So when Ruth recommended Elissa attend Ponca Pines, Elissa's mother complied.

CHAPTER VIII

Alyssa

Alyssa found herself at Ponca Pines a few months before Elissa arrived, after being expelled from a coed therapeutic boarding school called Carlbrook. Before Carlbrook shuttered in 2015, its mission was the same as that of Ponca Pines and all the rest: social restoration—the practice of reforming wealthy, wayward teens, returning them to the straight and narrow, and in doing so, enabling them to reclaim their power and privilege. When Alyssa refused rehabilitation, she was kicked out and shipped off to another school to be fixed. Nebraska is one of the only states in the country where you're considered a minor until you're nineteen. Elissa's and Alyssa's parents had sent them to Ponca Pines just before their eighteenth birthdays—the age they'd be allowed to check themselves out of their respective schools in any other state—so they'd have a whole extra year to be restored.

Back in Providence, I'd lost track of Elissa. I was convinced that Elissa had lost interest in me, actively choosing not to update me on her whereabouts. I barreled even further into my wannabe hipster pursuits—taking to wearing oversized headphones around my neck, listening to The Smiths, The Shins, and The Strokes on repeat between classes—and making new friends who liked similar artists. Case in point, my classmate Catherine, whose battle with bulimia I became heavily involved in, employing my gift of consolation that sometimes felt like my own private superpower. My ability to handle talking to anyone about anything, no matter how deep or dark.

As I suspected, Elissa had also made a new best friend: Alyssa, her roommate at Ponca Pines. On the surface, they looked nothing alike. Elissa was short, stick thin, and had a face full of freckles. Alyssa was tall, with an hourglass figure and porcelain skin. Yet Alyssa knew from the moment Elissa stepped into their dorm room that first day that they were meant to be like sisters at Ponca Pines. There Elissa was, much like herself, a Jewish American princess.

Elissa and I had also proudly identified as JAPs, a pejorative, catchall label for materialistic, whiny, selfish girls. The Jewish version of a Valley girl, the exact opposite of the well-heeled female WASPs. We loved wearing "Jappy" attire like Tiffany charm bracelets and Chanel sunglasses. Throughout middle school I'd pair my velour sweats with a T-shirt that said *kvetch* in big, bold letters. Had I found a shirt with *JAP* written on it, I would've proudly bought that, too.

At Ponca Pines, Alyssa was happy to find someone she identified with. After getting kicked out of Carlbrook, she'd retreated even further inward as a means of survival. She'd begun to slouch her shoulders once again, hunching until she became concave. After Elissa's arrival, she relaxed, straightened.

The Troubled Teen Industry attracts many wealthy white kids from suburbs and socioeconomic classes like Alyssa's. While working-class, bad-behaving teens often enter the school-to-prison pipeline, the criminal justice system weeds out the wealthy. Not because teens of different socioeconomic backgrounds commit different acts of rebellion. For all intents and purposes, the rich and the poor are just as likely to drink, do drugs, and have sex. But economic status dictates the punishments these teens receive for their misdeeds. Girls like Elissa, Alyssa, and Alissa wound up at Ponca Pines for therapy, siloed away with other Jappy, Waspy, and upper-crust teens whose parents could afford the school's price tag.

Alyssa and Elissa's bond ran deeper than wealth. After a few short weeks of rooming together, Owen was no longer the only person who mattered to Alyssa. She granted Elissa access to the emotions she otherwise kept behind the barrier that no therapist her parents hired could penetrate.

"Do you remember the prayer for Shabbat?" Alyssa asked.

"Obviously. *Baruch atah Adonai, Eloheinu melech haolam, asher kid'shanu b'mitzvotav v'zivanu l'hadlik ner shel Shabbat.*"

"Dude, you could be, like, a rabbi."

"At least they get to fuck!"

Judaism bled into the everyday fabric of their bond, and the two used their limited knowledge of Hebrew words as part of their shorthand. Only 0.5 percent of Nebraska's population was Jewish, and as a result, nobody on staff could decipher what the girls meant when they slipped *boker tov* or *todah* or *sliha* into regular conversation. Elissa and Alyssa started capitalizing on their confusion. After a classmate referenced Hitler, they demanded a formal apology. They convinced the kitchen staff to purchase special soy milk, claiming that the whole milk was too much for their Jewish stomachs.

"I seriously think we could get away with anything if we told them we were doing it because we were Jewish," Elissa said.

"It's like they think they're being anti-Semitic if they get mad at us," Alyssa said.

"Seriously."

"Should we, like, ask to go to temple for Shabbat or something?"

"Ugh, but do we even want to go to temple?"

"It gets us off campus."

"True. But what's something we *actually* want?"

Alyssa and Elissa were cautious about who they went to with their request. Before Ponca Pines closed its doors in 2012—the official press release claimed that the issue was the *lack of a facility and not lack of support, or financial issues*—it was much smaller than the average therapeutic boarding school. It enrolled around a dozen teens, as opposed to Spring Ridge's fifty or Carlbrook's eighty, and had a more modest-sized administration than many others. There were a handful of counselors and teachers who, like at the other schools, did not hold degrees in psychology, but still were heavily involved in the girls' day-to-day treatment. As for psychiatric services, Ponca Pines had both an art and a behavioral therapist. And at the top of the pyramid was Ponca Pines' founder: Shirley.

Shirley was a slight woman with a shock of auburn hair. Before founding Ponca Pines, she'd spent years making a name for herself in the therapeutic boarding school sector. The Troubled Teen Industry is an entangled one. Its practitioners rarely spend their careers at one program. Instead, they'll move from a stint at a wilderness program to a bigger role at a therapeutic boarding school, working their way up the administrative track, making connections with fellow employees along the way. The lack of governmental oversight makes these relationships all the more essential. It's up to the employees to band together and protect their industry, working together to make sure it stays as it currently is: in the shadows.

The instant Maia Szalavitz's name became familiar to me, it became inescapable, popping up in article after article about the industry that pulls on her reporting from *Help at Any Cost* or her more recent op-eds about the future of addiction and harm reduction. When I reach her via phone one day, I'm refreshed by Maia's no-nonsense approach to discussing the industry. Often, as I read about the abuses students have suffered at these programs and the quack psychology many employ, I find myself seeking some larger answer as to why they still persist. Something that will make it all make sense. But, for Maia, it all seems to come back to a strange catch-22 rooted in the privilege and power of the industry. "The industry was targeting wealthy individuals. It was seen as, like, rich people, they can advocate for themselves.

There's no reason that this should be problematic. It's expensive, so it must be good," she tells me.

And over the years, the Troubled Teen Industry has enacted more formal networks. Groups like the National Association of Therapeutic Schools and Programs (NATSAP), a trade organization of troubled teen institutions that Shirley has sat on the board of. While NATSAP claims to be a managing body—a group that's meant to investigate abuses such as those of the 145 children that ProPublica found have died while in the care of the Troubled Teen Industry since 1980—it's a far cry from the type of reform Breaking Code Silence is advocating for. Instead, NATSAP exists as a veneer of regulation to stave off outside interference. Subterfuge so these programs can continue to profit off wealthy families with outsiders continuing to think, like Maia put it, *It's expensive, so it must be good.*

Most programs within NATSAP offer similar treatment models. Chief among them is a levels system. It's operant conditioning in action. Students must exhibit proof that they're trying to change in order to progress to the next level, and each new tier comes with rewards. At Ponca Pines, graduating from level one to level two meant that a student could have access to the phone. Get bumped up from level two to level three, and she was allowed to leave campus for designated outings. This levels model is a way to both chart a student's growth as well as incentivize them to modify their behavior.

Under Shirley's tutelage, if a student were to share in group therapy, she might get to check her Facebook messages, but if she were to talk back to a counselor, she might have to clean the toilets. While Ponca Pines' punishments were mundane, other schools got more inventive. Carlbrook required students to run around the campus carrying full jugs of water. At one Utah facility, teens were made to sit in a horse trough with contaminated water up to their torso.

To help determine a student's level, some schools place spies around the campus or task counselors with keeping an eye out for infractions. Students are often encouraged to report any misbehavior they observe, and their loyalty to the program can earn them quicker access to their next level. At the end of each month, Ponca Pines staff would take stock of the intel they'd gathered for the girls' evaluation.

Evaluations were among the only times the girls met with Shirley. Once a month, they would come before her and a small panel of Ponca Pines staff for a check-in. With their parents on speakerphone, the staff would detail the girls' progress. Much of Alyssa's evaluation centered on her lack of participation in classes and therapy. Her unwillingness to speak up or to dig deep in therapy was unacceptable. After a forty-five-minute discussion about each student's successes and shortcomings, they'd give their ruling about whether the student was inching closer to graduating and being successfully socially restored or if she was moving in the wrong direction, toward punishment and loss of privileges.

When it came time for Elissa and Alyssa to play the Jew card, they knew better than to go to Shirley. Instead, they went to their counselor Jess, who allowed them to watch *The Colbert Report* clips on Fridays and brought in surprises like Japanese peppers—rewarding the girl who revealed herself to have the highest heat tolerance with a Snickers bar.

"Jess, have you ever heard about this super weird Jewish rule?" Elissa asked.

"It's random, but really important," Alyssa chimed in.

"What is it?" Jess inquired.

"I think it says it in the Torah or something. That if there're two Jews, neither of them can be closer to God," Alyssa said.

"Yeah, so me being on the top bunk is making my OCD insane because it's, like, so not okay," Elissa said.

"What do you want me to do about it?" Jess asked.

"Can we do some rearranging?" Elissa replied.

"Sure, whatever you girls need to do," she responded.

The girls retreated to the school's main house, where the dorms were located. Like I saw during my trip to Ponca Pines, the campus is small, consisting of a double-wide trailer where classes were held, a gym, and the residence itself. The house was originally built in 1918 and was set back amid the untended, wooded ravine that bordered the property. When Ponca Pines acquired the land in 2008, they converted the home into a five-thousand-square-foot, emphatically homey academy, remodeling the basement into a serene therapeutic studio, the dine-in kitchen into an intimate cafeteria, and the bedrooms into dorm rooms designed to fit two people, two built-in desks, and one set of bunk beds. So when Alyssa and Elissa ripped their twin XL mattresses off their designated bunks, laying them parallel to each other on the ground, they took up the vast majority of the floor space, bumping up against the desks, resting under the large window that looked out at the whole of the school. The residence was only a stone's throw away from the school's other facilities, and from their bedroom they could take in the totality of the land. The trailer where the girls would meet for four-hour blocks of class, often taking college courses on laptops in lieu of a traditional lecture. The field in front of it, which held a lone swing set and a wooden bench that sat at the edge of the grass before the land dipped off into the mess of tall grass and overgrown trees. A whole ecosystem in just a few acres.

Once Alyssa and Elissa's renovation was approved and completed, their dorm became the go-to lounge for the other girls. Like Lexi, a side-banged brunette from Louisiana who lived a few rooms over. Sprawling on the floor, they'd make fun of Lexi for being Christian. *You really believe in hell? Do you think Jewish people had horns? Jesus is kinda hot*, they'd tease.

Though Alyssa was happy in her room talking to the girls, she still struggled at Ponca Pines during therapy or when prompted to open up about her issues. Melody, Ponca Pines' therapist, was the first person to get Alyssa to participate. Unlike Shirley, she hadn't come from another therapeutic boarding school. Her background was in narrative therapy, and while she was required to lead them in group therapy, she approached their sessions with a sense of humor and an overall ease. Alyssa had taken to making friendship bracelets. All day she'd braid together different brightly colored pieces of string to help steady her nerves. And Melody encouraged this, allowing her to fiddle with the string during their afternoon group sessions.

Each session would begin with Melody offering the group an icebreaker.

"How do you feel?" Melody asked.

"Tired," Lexi answered.

"Cranky," Halle said.

"Perturbed," Elissa said. It was the same descriptor she picked every session, taking pleasure in how much it sounded like *pervert*.

After the icebreaker, Melody would share the therapeutic exercise of the day. Oftentimes these focused on building healthy relationships. Alyssa wasn't the only one with a complicated romantic past. Halle had lost a boyfriend to suicide. Charlotte had struck up a relationship with a heroin dealer. Whereas I'd yet to have a boyfriend, going relatively unnoticed by the many boys I had blindingly unrequited crushes on. And even if they had liked me back, I wouldn't have believed it, still identifying as that ugly girl Elissa had labeled me so many years before.

Melody's approach was nontraditional. Once, she asked the girls to read excerpts from Greg Behrendt's 2004 *He's Just Not That into You* and discuss how it reflected their experiences. Another time she asked them to draft "male scales": a list of twenty-five different things that they did and did not want in a partner. She understood that whom the girls chose to surround themselves with after Ponca Pines would be paramount to their success in the real world. Usually the Troubled Teen Industry's therapeutic practices were similar to the type of group sharing you'd see in a twelve-step program—various people huddled together in a haphazard circle, sharing their secrets—rather than the bespoke care she provided. But given that in the United States, there are almost no rules about the type of mental health care these programs provide, Melody was free to implement new lessons as she saw fit.

Spring Ridge, Carlbrook, and many of the other schools' curricula incorporated group therapy exercises that pitted students against each other, like a more experimental version of attack therapy. One such exercise asked students to pick three members from their group that they would save from drowning on an imaginary lifeboat. As the activity continued, it became a game of musical chairs, with the students running around as the spots on the raft dwindled and dwindled, until they were emotionally and physically exhausted enough to begin to verbally fight over the remaining spots as if they were actually their only means of survival. Alyssa, who had survived her fair share of lifeboat-like exercises, was grateful for Melody's more laid-back approach, even if she didn't quite see the merits.

"Who's ready to share?" Melody asked after the girls had completed their scales.

"I'll go," Halle offered.

"Great," Melody said.

"He can't wear a wifebeater. And he definitely can't call or text me too much," Halle read off.

"That's so annoying when they do that," Charlotte said.

"Right?" Halle said.

"They have to be obsessed with me," Elissa said, in jest.

"Honestly, Owen checks all my boxes," Alyssa said.

"What do you mean?" Melody asked.

"He's my soul mate," Alyssa said.

"But what about him? What boxes does he check?" Melody replied.

Alyssa paused; she'd received this line of questioning before. From her mother, her therapists in Northbrook, the various programs she'd attended. No adults got her and Owen, so what was the point of spelling it out for them?

"Literally every single one," she said.

It would've been easy for Alyssa to renounce Owen. To claim that she was no longer interested in him, that thanks to her treatment she'd seen the light. Owen served as the perfect representation of everything that was wrong with her, from her drug use to her emotional dependency issues. Many adults in her life subscribed to the idea that if Alyssa stopped seeing Owen, her damage would disappear with him. They were unaware of how far beyond Owen her demons extended. Unaware of all the danger that was awaiting Alyssa after graduation, unrelated to her relationship.

All around Alyssa students were doing this: putting their heads down, doing the work, admitting to their wrongdoing to get out of the program. But when it came to Owen, Alyssa wouldn't relent.

"I'm going back to him the second I get out of here," she said.

"Sounds like your mind is made up," Melody said.

"The second I turn nineteen," Alyssa said.

CHAPTER IX

Alissa

After a few months, Alissa hardly recognized herself in the Ponca Pines uniform: khaki pants and a forest-green polo. She fixated on the way the khaki pants billowed at her hips, how the polos accentuated her shoulders. When Elissa and I were in middle school, we'd put our legs together to see if our thighs, knees, or ankles touched. The more gaps, the hotter our bodies. In the Ponca Pines khakis, Alissa grew convinced that even her ankles were inching closer together. Her face appeared foreign to her as well. She typically wore makeup and would trace her bottom and top eyelids in black liner that she smudged for effect. The heavy eyeliner would draw people right to her aquamarine eyes. But the girls on the lower levels weren't allowed to wear makeup. It was a privilege.

Alissa started at Ponca Pines shortly after Alyssa and Elissa. It was a fifteen-mile jaunt with her mother from West Omaha to the remote, rural pocket of the city where the school was located.

They drove down Calhoun Road, passing farms, untended pastures, and dehydrated grass. Many therapeutic boarding schools exist in these isolated types of neighborhoods. Spring Ridge called Mayer, Arizona, home: a hamlet of a town with a population of 1,500-odd residents. Carlbrook's campus was in Halifax, Virginia, a community consisting of just 3.8 square miles. The farther away from civilization the schools were, the better their ability to remain clandestine, out of sight, out of mind.

Soon after Alissa's arrival, she was invited to join the girls in the kitchen for a snack. Mealtime was many of the girls' favorite. They were able to use their school-sanctioned allowances to buy groceries, filling the cabinets with trail mix, cheese puffs, and candy bars. Occasionally they were also allowed to cook, with Elissa, Alyssa, and the others banding together to make their iteration of a fruit salad: Cool Whip, canned pineapples, and preserved mandarins.

One of the first people Alissa spoke to was Charlotte, a curly-haired brunette with thin, rounded eyebrows. In the beginning of our conversations, Charlotte couldn't remember much about her time at Ponca Pines. While she's now in law school and the mother of two young daughters, her first few years after graduating were full of physical altercations and arrests. Charlotte had repressed many of these years up until we started talking, and they began bubbling back up to the surface. Our conversations reignite her long-buried grief as she laments to me, "*I don't have any Elissas left.*"

But back when Charlotte first met Alissa, they sat next to each other at the kitchen's oversized community table by the large windows looking out on the woods. The two made small talk, introducing themselves to each other, but Charlotte was too pre-occupied by the way Alissa barely tended to her meal to fully take in what Alissa was saying. Young women are the demographic most at risk for eating disorders, and there are a series of subtle behaviors that indicate if someone might be suffering.[1] I learned many of these during my friendship with Catherine: How she'd often choose to stand rather than sit. Or how other girls I knew who struggled would practice "body checking," the act of staring at yourself in the mirror, repeatedly weighing yourself, or mea-suring your limbs to reassure yourself you're still thin. Or being obsessed with eating only a small, select group of things: an apple, a cup of cottage cheese, cucumbers sliced thin. As Charlotte observed Alissa exhibiting her own version of these behaviors, she grew increasingly anxious.

"Don't worry, I'm not, like, a narc... But I can tell what you're doing," Charlotte blurted out. While Charlotte could be blunt, she was rarely cruel. The register of her voice is still a soft, pre-ternaturally cheery tone that offsets the harshness of any of her comments.

"What do you even mean?" Alissa replied.

"I used to do it, too."

"I seriously have no idea what you're talking about."

"You haven't had, like, any of your food."

"I'm so full."

"Your plate's... full."

In 2007, the BBC show *Skins* aired and taught a generation of young women how to avoid getting caught not eating. The show's anorexic main character, Cassie, demonstrates to her love interest how she hides her habit. Chopping up her meal into tiny pieces, moving it around the plate, complimenting it, offering her table-mate a bite. Anything to keep the person across from her distracted. Alissa would also spend meals pushing her food around, feigning consumption.

When Charlotte was in fifth grade, she and her friends had a contest to see who could eat the least. One by one, they dropped off. But Charlotte found herself really liking it. Her empty stomach churning like the low, steady beat of a washing machine. The hunger tugging at her, both a nuisance and an anchor. Charlotte claimed she didn't quite know what she was doing. She just knew that food was no longer appetizing to her. All she craved was that emptiness. Then, when Charlotte was eleven, her body gave out. She was admitted to the ICU, and after being discharged, she spent the next two years in an outpatient treatment facility. Despite her time there, the eating disorder didn't truly abate; it clutched to her, never fully withdrawing. Alissa posed a threat to Charlotte's recovery.

"Look, I got you. I get it."

"Okay, I guess."

"Let's start tonight. Just take, like, one bite. That's all you gotta do."

"I dunno."

"I told you. Trust me."

Charlotte started giving Alissa small lessons in nutrition, urging her to load up on multigrain toast with peanut butter, to reintroduce healthy fats back into her diet, encouraging her to take a few more bites of cereal, a food bland enough that it wouldn't upset her stomach. Alissa followed her advice. As the youngest in her family, she was used to being told what to do. In addition to her mother, her older sister had always heaped guidance on her.

"Put a shit ton of Nutella on there," Charlotte said to Alissa during a snack break.

"Ugh. That has so many calories," Alissa said.

"Girl, it's good for you. It's natural."

"Are you serious?"

"You see me eating it, don't you?"

Deep down Alissa didn't want to start eating again. For Charlotte, or for anyone else. She liked the way her disease had changed her body. Hollowing her belly, sinking her cheeks, flattening her breasts. This paradox is something that Kelsey Osgood writes about in the 2013 *How to Disappear Completely: On Modern Anorexia*. Claiming that while nobody delights in the bloating of alcoholism or the pock and track marks that plague drug addicts, with anorexia, the outward effects are often celebrated. Despite anorexia having the highest mortality rate of any psychiatric disorder, society praises the fruits of starvation. The waif, heroin chic, the Kate Moss effect. To Alissa, looking like this was all that mattered.

"I feel so fucking fat," Alissa said one night. Counselors roamed the hallways—in the Troubled Teen Industry there is often someone on guard, waiting to catch you misbehaving and properly punish you for it. Alissa spoke softly enough not to rouse them.

"I get it. I hated gaining weight in the beginning. It was, like, disgusting," Charlotte said.

"No, seriously. I'm, like, morbidly obese."

Alissa's weight on the scale had increased since she started eating Charlotte's way. The increase was so small that it could be attributed to water weight, but still, it consumed her mentally. She started to envision rolls, flab, jowls. She wanted to get better but hated seeing any signs of progress.

"Yeah, okay."

"Whatever. I just feel shittier than ever."

"What do you mean?"

"I just fucking hate my body."

Anorexia is more than twice as common in teenage girls as in any other age-group.[2] And while it's impossible to determine the psychological root of the disorder, there are certain factors that can cause the disease to flare up. Chief among them is emotional distress. In *Appetites*, Knapp writes, "When you're starving, or wrapped up in a cycle of bingeing-and-purging, or sexually obsessed with a man, it is very hard to think about anything else, very hard to see the larger picture of options that is your life, very hard to consider what else you might need or want or fear were you not so intently focused on one crushing passion." And as Ponca Pines had isolated Alissa, taken away her ability to communicate with the outside world, and stolen any sense of her autonomy—inflicting her own pain became the ultimate coping mechanism.

"You used to throw up all the time, right?"

"Yeah..."

"How do you do it?"

"I'm not gonna tell you that."

"Why not?"

"Because, honestly, you really need to gain some weight."

"C'mon."

"Girl, they'll keep you here forever if you don't."

Though Charlotte refused to teach Alissa the ways of bulimia, it wasn't too difficult to figure out. Once Alissa figured out how to make herself throw up, she reveled in it. Just as my younger sister did, having successfully become bulimic where I had failed. Though Jordan recovered, she still recalls the act of placing her index and middle fingers far in the back of her throat, farther back than it felt comfortable to go, until her knuckles grazed the ridges of her front teeth, and her saliva briefly became saline, before turning to acid. Showing me the places where her teeth punctured her skin, leaving scars behind on her fingers that she now hides with gold rings.

For Alissa, bulimia was a necessary evil. The counselor had started to notice that she never seemed to finish her plate. Watching over her at meals, seeing to it that her food was being eaten. To avoid discipline, she had to supplement starvation with bingeing and purging and rampant exercise.

After classes finished for the day, the girls would spend the late afternoon at the gym: toying with the weights, jogging on the various cardio machines. Alissa went on the elliptical, electrified by the machine's promise to help burn the most body fat in the shortest amount of time. She'd strap her feet into the pedals, grasping at the handles, willing them to move faster. The small electronic tracker that sat above the handles counted her mileage, pace, and calories burned. Afterward, she'd brag about the numbers she'd hit to Charlotte. The next day she'd set new challenges for herself to go faster, shed more. The tracker kept ticking on, going from 300 calories to 350 to 375.

Ponca Pines started to impose frequent weigh-ins. A staffer would pull Alissa aside unexpectedly and bring her to a private room to weigh her. Though tracking weight is a necessary measure in eating disorder recovery, the debate over whether or not to inform the patient of their weight is a heated one. Because for young women already predisposed to compulsive, obsessive thinking, having a number to fixate on can sometimes do more harm than good. For Alissa, the lack of lost weight and her disappointment in herself was a double-edged sword.

"We're not seeing any change," Shirley said to Alissa after one weigh-in.

"I'm sorry," Alissa said.

"Something's going to need to change."

"I'll do better."

"How are we supposed to trust you to do that?"

"I know, I know."

"No more gym privileges."

"What?"

"You'll use that time to focus on schoolwork."

"Isn't working out healthy? Isn't the whole point of this that I'm supposed to get healthy?"

"Prove to us that you can get healthy."

Operant conditioning demands that for each deviation from the rules, there must be an equal punishment. In the Troubled Teen Industry there's usually a penalty for bad behavior. Elissa once got written up after picking her nose in front of her class-mates for a laugh. Alyssa was denied moving up a level because she'd refuse to speak in class. For Alissa, they restricted her from the gym.

She resented the afternoons alone in the dorms. She'd flip through her textbooks, disinterested and angry that she wasn't in the gym sweating onto the handles, pedaling fast enough to hit her metrics. The anger she felt at the staff was overwhelming. She convinced herself she was growing sedentary, gaining weight with each second that she sat.

Anorexia is among the most difficult of mental health condi-tions to treat, with 30 percent of patients never recovering. Alissa fell squarely into that statistic. After Ponca Pines, she continued to struggle with her drinking. Sobering up and shedding the bloat. Falling off the wagon and puffing up from the sugar all over again. Restricting and shaming and purging herself all the while—sober, drunk, or otherwise.

But in recent years, there's been a new leading form of anorexia treatment. The Maudsley Approach is an intensive, three-phase, outpatient program that encourages families to play an active role in the patient's recovery, from taking over the eating schedule to accompanying them to therapy.[3] As the Maudsley Approach is used more and more, other treatments have fallen out of favor. Enrolling teen girls in inpatient eating disorder programs has become a discredited practice, as has employing operant condi-tioning on patients. This approach has proven that it's harmful to remove privileges from teen girls, only giving them back once they've gained weight. It's also shown that there is little evidence that group therapy is beneficial for girls with anorexia—in fact, it can worsen their condition.[4]

The Troubled Teen Industry's approach to treatment is largely homogeneous. No matter what malady a student is grappling with—drug addiction, depression, anorexia, et cetera—they must attend the same group therapy. There's rarely individualized treatment. The girls are held to the same healing benchmarks. The levels system, behavior modification, communal therapeutic exercises, and daily schedules are meant to provide one-size-fits-all healing, regardless of a student's experiences, trauma, or vice. Shortly after Alissa lost gym-time privileges, she was no longer allowed to visit the bathroom until thirty minutes after eating. One by one her privileges dwindled, while her self-flagellating thoughts remained.

CHAPTER X

Elissa

Elissa was boy-crazy and boys were crazy about her. In Providence, there had always been a boy in line ready to be the next star of her attention. Justin, the short, Italian American baseball player. Cole, a skater-surfboarder with shaggy bangs who lived in Brooklyn, but whom she'd met on AIM through a mutual friend. They were fleeting, all-consuming romances. Elissa would get a quick dopamine rush from one and then she'd rant and rave to me about the next.

Yet at Spring Ridge, Elissa had started exploring her sexuality—channeling the same compulsion I'd observed toward the three girlfriends she now juggled at once. Liz, a red-headed girl with a face full of freckles and a square jaw that made her appear undeniably butch. Cassie, a tall, milky-skinned, mousy brunette. Alexa, a petite platinum blonde. Liz, Cassie, and Alexa all thought they were Elissa's one and only—and Elissa basked in their unmitigated, complete desire for her. Romantic relationships are usually forbidden at therapeutic boarding schools. Elissa forged her relationships in secrecy.

The Troubled Teen Industry has a thorny relationship with queerness. There's a large faction of the industry that's associated with Christian organizations, which some parents send their children to solely for being gay. Networks such as Teen Challenge, which comprises over thirteen hundred centers and is affiliated with the Pentecostal Assemblies of God church, are religious programs known to employ conversion therapy: the pseudoscientific treatment where practitioners attempt to cure a patient of their sexual orientation or gender identity, aiming to realign the kid with heterosexual or cisgender norms. But even troubled teen facilities that are secular in nature, like Spring Ridge and Ponca Pines, may have conversion-like programming baked into their studies.

At Spring Ridge, Ruth was dogmatic about the girls being "ladylike." She kept a watchful eye over them to ensure they were living up to this expectation. Yet what brought Elissa's relationships to light wasn't Ruth's policing; it was hubris. She had befriended Brittany, a sensitive, soft-spoken girl who hated running the required morning laps, the same as Elissa. Brittany and Elissa's friendship developed while jogging in the back of the pack, chitchatting and half-assing their exercise. But when Elissa told Brittany about her girlfriends, she wasn't having it. Her slow pace was the extent of her defiance. Brittany took the program seriously, found the group therapy helpful, and was putting in the work to gain back privileges. Her loyalty was to the program.

"I'm sorry. It was nothing personal," Brittany said to Elissa a few days later, once it had become clear that Brittany had ratted her out.

"I get it, but, like...why then?" Elissa said in a whisper as they ran their customary laps.

"I could ask you the same question. You know you're not supposed to be hooking up with anyone."

"I just like to do the stupid things that I like to do."

"Dude, you gotta do better than that."

Elissa was placed on what Spring Ridge called S-N-S, which means "silence and separation," a punishment where students are banned from speaking, making eye contact, touching, or even being near certain classmates. According to Hannah, who spent four years at SRA, Elissa's S-N-S was among the most severe she ever saw the school issue. Elissa wasn't just prohibited from talking to Liz, Cassie, and Alexa—she was temporarily on S-N-S from the entire student body.

Drastic measures of discipline are not uncommon for queer students in the Troubled Teen Industry. At other schools, they'll refer to it as "Relationship Restriction." Students have spoken out about being required to act as if the person they're prohibited from speaking to no longer exists. Passing them in the hall without exchanging any looks, sitting on the side opposite them in class. And as BuzzFeed has reported, in some cases, these restrictions are issued as a preemptive strike. Used to prevent girls who are queer—or appear queer—from communicating with one another, just in case.[1]

Elissa made light of her sentencing, communicating with her friends via physical cues, like spraying a water bottle in their direction in the dining hall. She refused to let Ruth and the administration see her spirit dampened. But Elissa couldn't find any levity in the punishments Liz endured. After their relationship came to light, Liz was ridiculed for what they called her *tomboy* style. They urged her to dress more femininely and to start wearing nail polish. Her visible queerness posed a threat to her success at Spring Ridge.

The Troubled Teen Industry, like upper-class society, is extremely image based. If students look the part of the consummate straight, cisgendered, refined suburbanite, it's easy to convince parents that their children have been properly rehabilitated. Elissa's femininity seemed to spare her some of Ruth's wrath. Saved by her long hair, perfectly tweezed eyebrows, and penchant for lip gloss.

Once enrolled at Ponca Pines, Elissa approached relationships with her classmates with greater caution. While she still hungered for the high of romantic connection, she settled for cheap thrills. Elissa and Alyssa had started branching out. They'd befriended Alissa and Charlotte, taking turns hanging out in one another's dorm rooms. While all four got along, Elissa and Charlotte had the most playful relationship. Together they would up the ante on the commonplace flirting that often occurs between even the most platonic of female friends, me and Elissa included. The kind of ogling over each other's appearance—*your boobs in that dress! I wish I had your ass!*—that's tinged with latent eroticism. The playful teasing that men fantasize about happening at all-female sleepovers, despite the absence of the male gaze at Ponca Pines.

"Char, get over here with that booty," Elissa said.

"Coming for you, E Money," Charlotte replied.

"Ohhhh shit. Back that ass up."

Drake's *Thank Me Later* emanated from Charlotte's iTouch, an approved piece of technology at Ponca Pines as long as its content met their standards. Rap decidedly did not, but Charlotte had buried the album somewhere deep in the iPod's encryption, playing it while hanging out with Alissa, Alyssa, and Elissa in the latter two's dorm room. Charlotte was great at twerking, a skill she'd regularly show off to the other girls. And as "Show Me a Good Time" turned into "Up All Night," Elissa attempted to twerk alongside Charlotte. She lacked the rhythm to gracefully thrust her hips, not getting enough traction going to sustain continuously popping her butt up in the air. After two choruses' worth of Elissa's failed twerking attempts, Charlotte started grinding up on her.

"Get it, girl," Alissa cheered.

"Miss New Booooooooty," Alyssa bellowed.

"Ow ow," Elissa said, laughing along.

Soon enough, Elissa, Charlotte, Alyssa, and Alissa were rarely apart. The campus was small, and the corner of the residence where the dorms were housed was even smaller, made up of just a handful of bedrooms and adjoining bathrooms. Crammed into such close corridors, the girls rarely had a moment to themselves. When one showered, someone else would usually be peeing in the same bathroom, or standing above the toilet, stealthily smoking cigarettes out of the lone small window. There was one single-occupancy room on the floor, but that was reserved for girls who were new to the program. A temporary space to stay while the staff was getting room assignments sorted out. Until Lucie was placed there.

Lucie had a natural beauty. She had a honey-colored tan that lasted all year long, spindly limbs, and deep green eyes. Lucie didn't bother hanging out with the other girls on the swing set between classes or gossiping with them in one another's rooms. She preferred to keep to herself, to her dorm. I found this to be true in my limited interactions with her, exchanging a few messages with Lucie on Facebook—some in which she comes across as hostile, others a bit softer—before she stops responding to me altogether.

As a result, few of Lucie's classmates were eager to talk to her. The girls explained that her tendency to glare at the other girls irritated them, as did the way she'd snap at the staff or refuse to make eye contact. But her defiance amused Elissa. She'd become less outwardly obstinate since arriving at Ponca Pines, but still revered the quality in others. Lucie's single shared a bathroom with Alyssa and Elissa's room and the two started spending more time together.

Elissa could get quite annoying when she had a crush. In the early days of her relationship with Cole, he told her he'd been signed to a professional skateboarding league, had done a photo shoot for the cover of a surfing magazine, and had apprehended a terrorist on a flight. None of which was true, but Elissa believed it, adamantly defending him to me when I tried to question his stories. She assigned magical qualities to Cole; she thought he was truly capable of stopping the next 9/11. And this was the attitude Elissa developed toward Lucie, deifying her with the same force.

Elissa gravitated toward Lucie. Snagging the desk next to her as they took their online courses in the trailer, playing footsie with her beneath the long oak table where the girls dined family style.

"Gimme a bite of your hummus," Elissa said.

"Nooo. You have your own," Lucie replied.

"But I want some of youuuurs."

"Oh, stop it."

Though Elissa never spoke of her sexuality to the other girls—and it was something she hadn't previously spoken about with me either—Lucie's effect on Elissa was palpable. Elissa's hazel eyes flitting around the room, unable to steady until they landed on Lucie. Love was Elissa's coping mechanism, the outlet by which she seemed to derive feelings of comfort. A relationship to romance, I see now, that was less in keeping with the harmless, hormonal nature of boy-craziness, and much more in line with sex and love addiction: a mental disorder characterized by an inability to engage in healthy emotional intimacy.

According to research from the National Institutes of Health, addiction to sex and love elicits the same feelings of exhilaration, craving, and obsessive patterns of thought that are triggered by any other vice.[2] Sex and drugs even share neurochemical effects, both stimulating the same dopamine release in the nucleus accumbens.[3] Before meeting Lucie, Elissa had been in withdrawal, desperate for the physiological relief that came only from having someone to desire, and in turn to be desired by.

"Bathroom tonight?" Elissa asked once the two had a moment alone.

"You're so bad," Lucie said.

"Isn't that why you like me?"

"You're the worst."

After everything that had happened at Spring Ridge, Elissa had really tried to remain celibate. But sex had taken on a mythical element. It made her feel happy, good enough, whole.

Every night, Jess or another on-call attendant made the rounds, pacing aimlessly up and down the corridors, listening for even the slightest stirring. The residence was located far enough back in the woods that no outside noise poured in from the street. As Charlotte remembers it, the plan Lucie made was a rough one—meet in the bathroom, hope for the best—and Elissa lay there, listening to Jess's footsteps. Up and back, down the hall, then back up again. Elissa resting motionless in bed, seized by her anticipation.

"You came," Lucie said once in the bathroom.

"That's what she said," Elissa said.

"Shut up."

"Make me."

The shower took up a large portion of the bathroom's square footage: a walk-in stall, large enough for two people. But even in the privacy of the bathroom, Elissa and Lucie ducked behind the curtain to fool around. It had been hours since the shower had been used, and the floor was dry, coated in a sea of stubble and washed-off dirt. Elissa and Lucie tried to stay as still as possible while they kissed, their feet firmly planted in the debris.

Pressed up against Lucie, Elissa was gripped by a crescendo of emotions. Her brain's dopamine receptors were activated, filled with ecstasy, calm, and nirvana. Until Jess swung the bathroom door open, finding the girls in the shower, with Elissa's high swung to an all-time low.

"Girls! To your rooms. Now," Jess said.

"We were just...," Lucie attempted.

"We'll be dealing with you both in the morning."

———

One afternoon after the shower incident, the girls were almost done with class when they were asked to remain in the trailer. At Ponca Pines, the students had already been subjected to the school's version of attack therapy. On Sundays, they'd all gather in the residence's great room and go around in a circle, telling one another what they needed to work on. Compared to Spring Ridge, Elissa found the weekly exercise to be tame. Most girls just told the others that they were too bossy, or that they had an attitude problem. Skin-deep criticisms, barely penetrating the surface level of one another's insecurities. But on that afternoon, Jess entered the trailer and introduced a new, final lesson for the day. One that drew blood.

"Take a piece of paper and pass the rest down," Jess told the girls.

"We know what's been going on," she continued.

Jess didn't name anything outright; instead, she let her words hang in the air, watching as the girls made fearful eye contact with each other. Elissa staring at Lucie and the others, silently pleading with them to stay mum about whatever they'd gleaned of their relationship.

"Remember why you're here: to break these behaviors," Jess said while passing out pencils and instructing them to each compile a list of others' transgressions.

"We wouldn't want to see you get bumped down," Jess concluded.

"Time to hand them over," Jess said once she saw enough scrawl on each of the girls' pages.

"See, doesn't that feel better?" she asked as she collected them.

Though Elissa could only see the inky traces of writing on the pages of her surrounding classmates, there were enough words on the paper to confirm her suspicions. The girls had sold one another out. Charlotte had spilled everything she'd deduced about Elissa and Lucie's relationship. Some admitted to things that otherwise never would've been found out, so frenzied by the ordeal that they couldn't stop themselves from purging their wrongdoings. Jess stood in the front, reading through these confessionals, while the girls were left to sit silently in the wreckage of their allegiances.

At the exercise's conclusion, Jess excused the girls so she could further examine their confessionals, and a group of them gathered on the swings. Elissa lay on the grass in front of them, looking up at the sky in lieu of making any eye contact. But Lucie was incensed, and eager to unleash her anger. Pacing around in front of the swing set, ignoring Elissa as she laid into the others.

"So who's the snitch?" Lucie asked, looking at all the girls.

"I know one of you said something," she continued.

"We don't even know what anyone wrote down yet," Elissa said, trying to neutralize the situation.

"Yeah. We don't even know what *you* wrote," Halle said.

"This is bullshit," Lucie said, marching off.

Ultimately, Elissa and the others who had their secrets revealed were bumped down a level. Stripped of the privileges they'd become accustomed to. It was demoralizing, moving backward, not forward. But the greatest effect was on Elissa and Lucie's relationship itself, with the two of them never recovering, let alone maintaining a friendship.

Charlotte and Halle both remember how sad Elissa seemed in the weeks that followed. Dejected, despondent. It's painful for me to hear about Elissa appearing so outwardly distraught. Her poker face that she always maintained, even while in the hot seat, nowhere to be seen. While I'd glimpsed her rawest, most exposed nerves, these displays were typically reserved for our late-night talks. Never for public consumption.

Imagining Elissa in such a state ignites an old desire. One that I've since begun working through in Al-Anon, a recovery program designed to help support the family and friends of alcoholics or addicts. My desire to be the *one* to help people heal. To be the *one* who can handle any confession, any emotion. An addiction like any other, growing more self-serving and more unmanageable with time.

Alyssa

Alyssa's eighteenth birthday fell on October 23, 2010, the same day as her classmate Allie's. Birthdays were always a big deal at Ponca Pines, and the girls awaited October 23 with an unparalleled furor. Ecstatic at the process of having not one birthday cake with dinner, but two.

Despite their shared birthdays, Allie and Alyssa weren't particularly close. Allie seemed to get along better with her pet betta fish, Mojo, than the other girls. She'd transferred to Ponca Pines from Island View, a Utah-based therapeutic boarding school. Though the school has since closed, in just under fifteen years, 219 emergency calls were placed to the local police department, some of them related to allegations of abuse, sex offenses, or suicide attempts.[1] While Allie was at Island View, she broke her foot. It's not uncommon for Troubled Teen Industry staffers to deny students medical care, despite the fact that the practice has led to both lawsuits and deaths, like in the case of Aaron Bacon, who died as a result of not being treated for acute peritonitis while at a wilderness program. (Bacon was also subjected to a litany of other abuses, such as going without food for eleven days and being denied a sleeping bag for two weeks, despite the average overnight temperature being thirty-two degrees.)[2] And when Allie went to the staff about her foot, they told her that she was an attention-seeker and refused to get her help until the break had become so severe that she required surgery. Though Allie much preferred Ponca Pines to Island View, she was quietly counting down the days until her birthday—and what she knew she'd do once that day came.

Taking in these admissions is as maddening as it is excruciating, imagining my best friend's final years, confined to such darkness. The stories Allie tells are not only of her injury, but also of the times she was locked in an eight-by-eight windowless isolation room, smeared with urine and fecal matter stains. Or the meds she was forced to take, with someone placing them in her mouth and watching until she swallowed. How they made her so tired that she couldn't stop herself from falling asleep in class, an act that would lead her to be placed back in the isolation room as her punishment. An experience that's not unique to Allie, as governmental protection and advocacy groups found instances of misuse and overuse of psychiatric medication during monitored visits of youth residential facilities. It's incomprehensible to me that there are so many who would inflict such torment on teenagers. That there are networks full of adults abusing kids in the name of tough love. That even considering the many people I talk to, I will never know the full extent of the abuse Elissa absorbed.

Not all staff who enter the Troubled Teen Industry come in with the aim of inflicting hurt on teenagers. There are some who are clearly in it for the money. Wanting to exploit the exorbitant price tags associated with these programs, not the students themselves. But then there are the ones who truly believe that hurting kids is helping them. That abuse and tough love go hand in hand. Often, these are people who were either put through the industry as teens, experiencing this tough love firsthand, or have worked at another facility and have bought into its merits. In talking about the pathology of such a person with Maia Szalavitz, the concept of the "dark triad" comes up: a psychological theory of personality where someone displays narcissistic, Machiavellian, and psychopathic tendencies. The traits I can only imagine would be required for a person to think that to hurt is to help.

But just as not all staffers in the Troubled Teen Industry are of the dark triad variety, not all of a student's experiences will be colored with abuse. At Ponca Pines, birthdays were a time of total celebration. And on Alyssa's, her parents made the trip from Northbrook to be with their daughter for the milestone. At the beginning of the visit, Louise and Richard were hopeful. The campus was welcoming. Particularly the residence's great room, which the staff had designated as the space for family visits, and had refurbished with beige walls, neutral tiled floors, and a sprawling fireplace. Ponca Pines was much more provincial than Carlbrook, with its big brick buildings modeled after the prestigious prep schools of the North, but there was something about its bespoke charm.

Taking her parents in, Alyssa diverted her eyes from them. It had been so long since she'd seen her parents, and in the months that had passed, Alyssa had channeled all her rage into villainizing them. All she could think about when she looked at them was how they'd sent her away from her home, her life, Owen.

The visit didn't last long. Though Louise and Richard came with the best of intentions, within a few hours of Alyssa's silent treatment, they retreated back to the hotel. Leaving Alyssa to go through the motions of the evening on autopilot—enjoying her cake and celebrating with Allie and the others while silently stewing.

"I'm so fucking over it here," Alyssa said once they were back in the dorms.

"Tell me about it," Elissa said.

"Think I could make it if I made a run for it?"

"What do you mean?"

"I'm eighteen now."

Alyssa opened the window, sticking her head out just enough to judge the building's height. If she were to jump, it wouldn't be too far a drop. It was just about hitting it right. Avoiding the gravel driveway, making it onto the grass.

"Am I doing this?"

"Don't leeeave me."

"Shit, I really think I'm doing this."

Alyssa was hoping the third time would be the charm. In between her escape from O'Hare and this current attempt at running away, she'd plotted one other foiled attempt at breaking free. From Carlbrook.

Carlbrook was a place of gentility. Where students were able to take Advanced Placement courses, enter dual-enrollment programs with various colleges, and often go on to notable universities. Of the people I've come to know over the years who went to therapeutic boarding school, an overwhelming majority attended Carlbrook. It was even the subject of a 2021 memoir, *Stolen*, by Elizabeth Gilpin, which exposed the undercurrent of peril beneath its veneer of refinement. Plagued with disappearances, like in 2010, when a student ran away from the campus, rumored to be heading to Danville, Virginia, or Durham, North Carolina, with nothing more than a small bag of clothes. Over a decade later, he remains missing. In 2012, another student made a break for it, carrying only a small black backpack. To this day, his whereabouts are also unknown.

At Carlbrook, Alyssa was often in trouble—her uniform was too tight on her breasts, which led many of the students to have crushes on her, and which caused her to be reprimanded for exhibiting "attention-seeking" and "flirtatious" behavior. Constantly in and out of suspension—during which she was made to sit silently in a room and complete therapeutic writing exercises in isolation—she was miserable. And though internet access was forbidden at the school, Alyssa still found a way online, using it to communicate with Owen, making a plan for him to drive the thirteen hours from Northbrook to Carlbrook to help her escape.

But unlike her time at O'Hare, luck wasn't on Alyssa's side at Carlbrook. The administration intercepted her messages, called her parents, and together they devised a plan to send her straight to Ponca Pines. Alyssa knew how far downhill things could go if she was caught running away from Ponca Pines, but she was still willing to risk it all. To return to Owen.

"I'll cover for you," Elissa assured her as Alyssa dangled one leg outside the window, bracing herself for impact.

"I love you so much," Alyssa said.

"I love you more."

"No way."

When Alyssa hit the grass instead of the gravel, it seemed like a good omen. Maybe, just maybe this would work for her. She didn't have much of a plan. Iowa borders Nebraska on its easternmost side and is about two miles from Ponca Pines. In the state she'd be considered a legal adult upon entrance, ensuring she couldn't be returned to Ponca Pines against her will. As she sprinted past the campus's gate, running past Calhoun Road's country homes and fields of tall grass, Alyssa kept her eyes open for any driver who looked amenable to hitchhikers, willing to go with whoever could take her closer to a state border.

Runaways are a rampant issue throughout the Troubled Teen Industry, one that they plan for in advance. It's likely another reason they choose remote locations. If there's nowhere to run to, there's a much smaller likelihood of escape.

Staffers sometimes put the fear of God in students about what will happen to them if they do attempt to flee. Reminding them that they have no money, means of communication, food, or supplies. That if they run, they're likely to be abducted or worse on the road. And for those who do try to leave and fail, they'll often lose their right to wear shoes or their standard uniform upon return. Instead, they're made to wear pajamas or other clothes that won't stand up to nature's elements. Jailbreak was still a risk they were willing to take.

Allie's mother had also traveled to Omaha to be with her on her birthday, with Allie's best friend in tow. After the on-campus festivities, the three of them went out to dinner in downtown Omaha. Allie had grappled with severe culture shock when she'd first arrived at Ponca Pines. After all her time in Island View's isolation room, Ponca Pines' eleven acres were nearly too expansive to behold. The ability to walk freely around the campus was a luxury that took her time to comprehend. Now out for dinner, flipping through the laminated pages of an actual restaurant menu, Allie was overcome with grief.

"I'm going to run to the bathroom for a sec," Allie said.

"Wanna wait until they take our order?" her mother asked.

"No. I'll be quick."

"Okay, sweetie."

Allie headed toward the back of the restaurant, past the bathroom, past the kitchen, until she was through the door and out in the alleyway. It had been years since Allie had been an autonomous person in the world. While Ponca Pines sometimes took the girls on field trips into Omaha, Allie was always following a leader. Having someone tell her where they were going, what would be going down there. Walking around the downtown completely alone was as exhilarating as it was destabilizing.

Eventually Allie got up the nerve to enter a convenience store, where the cashier took pity on her. Misty had lived in Omaha long enough to have heard of Ponca Pines and was discerning enough to distrust the institution. She helped Allie purchase a bus ticket to Denver, where she'd grown up, and supplied her with a hoodie, snacks, and a pack of Marlboro Smooths for the nearly eight-hour trip. Allie was getting ready to leave for the bus station when the cops showed up at the store, with instructions to take her to Ponca Pines. They'd apprehended Alyssa a few hours prior, still running aimlessly down Calhoun Road, no escape vehicle in sight.

"Allie, Allie, Allie," Jess said after the cop car had pulled down the driveway, depositing her back in the staff's care.

"Hi," she said, shrugging.

"You're the second one tonight."

"Are you serious? Who else?"

"You'll see."

Alyssa was already waiting in the trailer, sitting in one of the same desks she crouched in during the school day. The trailer was windowless, and even though it was the latest that Alyssa had ever been inside it, thanks to its artificial lighting, the classroom appeared as it did any other time of day. Sterile and unchanged.

"You too?" Alyssa asked Allie once Jess guided her through the door.

"Yup," Allie said.

"Girls. Enough," Jess said, silencing them. "Stand up, Alyssa. Down to your underwear, the both of you."

Alyssa rose from her seat, joining Allie, peeling off layer after layer. Strip searches are common practice in the Troubled Teen Industry. Much like intake for prisoners, when students arrive at school, they might be forced to strip naked, get patted down, and are sometimes subjected to a cavity search. Just one of the many

parallels between the prison system and the Troubled Teen Industry. Kenneth Rosen, author of the 2021 memoir *Troubled: The
Failed Promise of America's Behavioral Treatment Programs*, pos-
its it's these similarities that made him feel prepared for a life of
adult incarceration, rather than leading him to avoid such a fate.
"By the end of my time away I recognized a bliss associated with
handcuffs. Lockup and lockdown meant the familiarity of strip
searches, drug tests, isolation cells and men who handled me like
I was worthless."

Standing in front of the desks, their clothes pooled on the floor
as they cowered in their bras, Alyssa and Allie attempted to cover
their exposed flesh with their hands.

"Turn, turn. I need to see both sides."

"Keep turning. You too, Alyssa."

"Hands off, I need to see everything."

Jess approached Allie and Alyssa, combing through their hair,
lifting their bra straps, searching for any hidden mementos. While
Alyssa's body was revered, she'd never been entirely at ease in it.
Her breasts had come to define her quickly, and her mind hadn't
had time to catch up. Big-Boob Girl was still a role she played.
She'd laugh along as Allie teased her for being *one hundred pounds
and thirty of them titty meat.* Standing before Jess and Allie with
her breasts on display mortified her, taking her back to the early
days of puberty when she'd walk through her high school hallways feeling more displayed than desired.

"All right, we're done here. For now," Jess said.

"Can I, uh, put my clothes back on?" Alyssa asked.

"Yeah. Get dressed. We're heading back to the dorms."

Alyssa and Allie walked out of the trailer side by side, hovering behind Jess. Coming upon the residence, Alyssa kept her eyes on her dorm room window. It had been only a few hours since she'd sprinted away from of it, seized by hope. Once inside the dorms, she tried to reenter her room with a calculated nonchalance. But Elissa had no patience for pretense.

"You're back," Elissa said.

"Yup. Fuck me," Alyssa said.

"Is it rude if I say I'm happy?"

"Yes! Bitch."

"Okay, I'm *not* happy then."

"I can see your smile from here."

Not everyone has the experience of the Troubled Teen Industry that Allie and Alyssa shared. So hopeless that they were willing to put themselves in harm's way, risk future punishment, all in the pursuit of escape. There are many graduates I speak with who have come away from treatment feeling that they've been given a new lease on life. Those who feel they've truly been rehabilitated, healed. And those like Alyssa, Alissa, and Elissa, who unfortunately didn't live to say.

CHAPTER XII

Alissa

Alissa could always count on Alyssa and Elissa. She loved Elissa's absurd antics, like how she'd pick her nose in public as a bit, to rouse her from a foul mood. Alyssa was her nonjudgmental ear, the person she trusted to understand just how much she missed getting fucked up. But the more time Alissa spent with Halle, the more Halle became her mirror. Halle reflected the confounding, complex characteristics of her personality. The ones that Alissa hadn't been ready to confront.

The first time Halle was sent to Ponca Pines, she didn't make it through the door. Halle has a fiery streak—one that I've observed firsthand. When we first connected, long before my visit to Nebraska, where I spent an evening eating pizza on the floor of her apartment with her, Halle ripped me a new asshole. Questioning my motives, my understanding of the girls, my thoughts on the Troubled Teen Industry. Sniping at me until I satisfied her inquiries, leaving me trembling as well as curious. *Who was this hellstorm?*

When Halle pulled down Ponca Pines' driveway that initial day, she also didn't hesitate to unleash on her parents. Cursing and screaming at them until a staffer approached, welcoming her to the school. The rest happened in quick succession: Halle punched the staffer, prompting the cops to show up, who then carted her off to juvie. She remained there for a few months, until she was released and sent back to Ponca Pines for round two. Upon her return, Elissa and Alyssa greeted Halle with a homemade sign for her dorm room door. It read: *Don't punch anyone this time.*

Alissa empathized with Halle, how anger can metastasize, feeling simultaneously hot and itchy as it spreads through your body. The way violence can feel like the antidote, the physical expulsion of rage. Alissa and Halle were also both from Omaha, were the same age, and had friends in common. Having attended similar parties, running in like-minded circles. They started spending more time together, listening to Eminem's *Recovery* album. Alissa's favorite song off the album was "No Love," which she favored for its lyric *throw dirt on me and grow a wildflower.* She identified with its message of perseverance, rapping it incessantly. Halle and Alissa would pass hours on end like this, spitting bars, talking about Eminem's poeticism.

While home visits were traditionally reserved for girls much further along in the program, given that Halle and Alissa lived so close to the school, they were occasionally permitted to go home. Their access to the outside world made them hot commodities among the other girls. Especially since they were always down for the cause.

"Can you get this letter out to Owen?" Alyssa asked.

"Will you bring back some more cigs?" Charlotte begged.

"Ooh, for me too," Elissa said.

"Yeah, yeah we got you," Alissa said.

"Whatever you guys need," Halle agreed.

Alissa and Halle spent their off-campus visits funneling contraband in and out of the school. On one trip, Halle bought a prepaid cell phone for her and Alyssa to share. While Halle's first boyfriend had committed suicide, she was in a new relationship by the time she entered Ponca Pines. Alyssa and Halle would trade off turns on the flip phone, using T9 to text Owen and Halle's boyfriend, always hyperaware of how quickly the minutes dwindled on such phones, knowing full well that each text could be their last. But the best things that Alissa and Halle snuck in they made sure to save for each other. Like the Adderall Alissa brought back as a surprise just for Halle.

By my senior year, I was also no stranger to prescription pills. It started the previous summer when I'd attended a filmmaking program in Dublin through NYU. It was my first extended time away from home, and I was nervous. Plagued by debilitating anxiety and blackout panic attacks. I hadn't experienced those emotions since my childhood—around the time my parents divorced, and my umbilical cord reattached to my mother—yet they returned with a vengeance. Worried about me, my mother gave me a bottle of her 0.5 mg lorazepam. Those petite white pills she kept in the champagne-colored Judith Leiber pill case in her purse. The ones she'd dole out to me over the years, whenever I was on the precipice of an obliterating bout of panic.

In Dublin, I developed an annihilating crush on an older,

hipster boy named Campbell in the program who wore a nicotine patch and semi-pornographic screen-printed T-shirts. Trying to impress him, I told him about the pills. Which worked, far better than any of my other sheepish attempts at flirting. I spent that summer with Campbell learning more about pill popping than about the majesty of Fellini films from the program. How hard I should press down on a tablet so it would crumble into powder and not go flying off the table. That dollar bills make better snorting instruments than pieces of paper, a rookie mistake I made that led me to slice the thin tissue of my nostril. The amount I should ingest so the pills made me feel weightless, not sleepy. At night, Campbell and I would lie in his twin-sized dorm room bed, blitzed out, drawing lightning bolts on each other's arms in Sharpie.

After the summer, he returned to boarding school on the West Coast, and I went back to Rhode Island. We'd talk on the phone from time to time, but only late at night, when I'd snorted lorazepam, using my high as a half-baked excuse to call him. While I knew that, fundamentally, I shouldn't be abusing lorazepam— it wasn't like my guilty conscious had evaporated; my desire to impress Campbell had just drowned it out—I was able to convince myself that it was fairly harmless because I'd been around the drug my whole life, as my mother wasn't the only member of my family with a prescription. My grandmother had one, along with both of my aunts. According to a report on the sex and gender differences in substance use, women are far more likely to get and use prescription pills than men.[1] This is because women experience chronic pain and anxiety more often than men and are more inclined to seek help from clinicians for their conditions.

But just as women are prescribed pills at a higher rate, they abuse them at a higher rate as well. In 2020, the Survey on Drug Use and Health estimated that 9 million Americans abused or misused prescription pills within the year. More than half were women. Though this statistic is a glaring one, not all this abuse is rooted in addiction. Some is of the stereotypically suburban variety. Made up of women like the ones in my family—who have a fully stocked medicine cabinet, an ample pill case, and a penchant for mother's little helpers.

Alissa's contribution to this statistic, at the time, teetered off the edge of more commonplace misuse into something greater. The early onset of addiction her mother so feared. Sitting in Halle's dorm room, Alissa stared at the Adderall tablets she'd laid out on the desk. It had been a long time since she'd gotten high, and she could already feel the way the drug would move through her. It was like the placebo effect in action, how she tasted the phantom nasal drip of its amphetamine salts leaking down the back of her nose, entering her blood stream.

"Should we just do it here?" Halle asked.

"No time like the present," Alissa said.

"I knew I liked you."

"Same, girl."

Alissa gathered a series of different heavy objects—a shoe, a calculator, then a textbook—waving them in Halle's direction for approval. Halle shook her head at the first two, before finally nodding at the textbook, to which Alissa smiled in agreement.

"You have a dollar somewhere?"

"Yeah, I think in the drawer."

"Cool."

Alissa brought the textbook down onto the pills with just enough vigor that they shattered into shards, splaying across the table. Alissa flipped her hand on its side, using it like she was a waiter with a crumber—ushering the pills' splinters and surrounding debris into a mound in the center of the table. Then she took the textbook to the pills one more time, this time smashing the smaller pieces hard enough for them to seep out into light blue powder. Repeating the same gathering motion, Alissa brushed the powder into another tight pile.

"You have anything to cut them with?"

"I don't think so."

"Let's just get after it, then."

"Fine by me."

Halle rolled up the dollar bill, passing it back and forth between Alissa and herself as they took turns depleting the piles. With the bill plunged into Alissa's nose, its stench overpowered her. The familiar mix of cotton, ink, metal, and finger grease lingered in her nose, even as the Adderall traveled into her nasal membranes. That mucus-inducing, electrifying release she'd been waiting for. It didn't take long for Halle and Alissa to finish off the powder— the pills had just amounted to a few hits each—and before its effects even took hold, the girls were gripped by an anticipatory sadness. Already missing the feeling of being outside of themselves, out of their Ponca Pines existence, for just a few hours.

"What next?"

"Like we have so many options."

"Ugh."

Now high, Alissa had never felt so cramped in her room before. It was the first time she'd paid any attention to how manufactured the dorm was: its charmless bunk beds and décor-free walls. Intentionally void of personality, to suit her just as well as the girl who had been there before her, and the one who'd come after. Pacing around the room, Alissa became hyperaware of how much her tolerance had decreased since she'd been at Ponca Pines, which also made her anxious. She felt desperate for an outlet, something to channel all her excess energy into. Anything to upend her unease.

Alissa had never been a good student. Not at Ponca Pines, her public high school, or middle school before it. But in the clutches of her Adderall high, she did the one thing she hated above all else: homework. Alissa brushed the lingering powder off the desk and spread open her books. Speed-reading her textbooks, furiously jotting down notes, working on her various assignments. Over on the bunk beds, Halle started tackling her homework as well. Another common use for Adderall is as a study aid. It's how my classmates at Wheeler frequently took it: cramming for finals, hoping the pills would unlock that extra, untapped brain capacity. It became so prevalent among prep schools and universities for these purposes that our age-group has been deemed Generation Adderall. And though Alissa and Halle didn't intend to reap the studying benefits of the drug, they received them all the same.

The next day in class, Halle and Alissa presented the fruits of their labor. Alissa was nervous as she handed over her assignment. Scared that it was so obvious that *something* had transpired. That the effort she put into her homework would be all the evidence needed for them to realize she'd gotten high. Her confession, right there on the page.

"Alissa, this is some seriously great work here," their teacher, Carly, said as she skimmed over Alissa's paper.

"Really?" Alissa asked.

"Yes! Keep up the good work."

"I'll try."

Alissa took the compliment, smiling along as Carly praised her scholastic achievements. Now a few months into her stay at Ponca Pines, Alissa had gotten better at playing the part. Figuring out new ways to hide her eating disorder and to sneak around on her home visits. Fake compliance. The poker faces that Alissa and so many other students have perfected to succeed in the industry, acting according to the staff's expectations, telling their therapists what they want to hear, outwardly changing their behavior. One day, during group therapy, Charlotte claimed she'd seen the light and realized that weed was evil. After ending things with Lucie, Elissa started writing notes to the new girls who came to the school, telling them how much Ponca Pines had helped her, urging them to do well in the program. But both were faking their rehabilitation. Doing whatever was required of them to move through the levels system, earn back more privileges, and finally get closer to graduation.

The prevalence of fake compliance is just one of the many reasons why behavior modification programs have fallen out of favor as treatment for teens struggling with their mental health. In recent years, practices like cognitive behavioral therapy (CBT), dialectical behavioral therapy (DBT), parent management training

(PMT), collaborative assessment and management of suicidality (CAMS), and acceptance and commitment therapy (ACT) have risen in popularity. But among these approaches, experts have been increasingly recommending DBT as the preeminent treatment for teenagers faced with PTSD, bipolar disorder, schizophrenia, depression, or anxiety. Diagnoses many in the Troubled Teen Industry may suffer from—Elissa, Alyssa, and Alissa included.

As the *New York Times* outlined in "The Inner Pandemic," a 2022 multipart project exploring adolescent mental health, DBT focuses on reframing a person's thoughts and behaviors.[2] It's made up of four components: individual therapy for the teen, group therapy, and emotional regulation training for parents and their children, as well as phone access to their therapist for crisis intervention. The first step is teaching patients to identify the feelings in their body when a dangerous impulse arises. How their pulse might begin to hasten and race, their shoulders might buckle and lock. Patients are then instructed to put those feelings into words, which engages part of the brain, helping to regulate their emotions. The next step is to introduce techniques that reduce this arousal state. Jumping jacks, splashing cold water on your face, pressing ice to the body. Small, simple actions that reintroduce a state of calm, recentering the body and mind.

Amid the many merits of DBT, there's one core pillar of care that stands out to me the most. That parents are instructed to play an active role in the treatment. With teens not being sent away to receive this treatment—only seeing their families during visits or doing therapy with them over the phone—but with it happening in the community. Where parents can observe their recovery firsthand, being there for the highs and the lows, the crises and the breakthroughs.

Learning more about these treatments, all I can think about is the extent to which the girls' parents were deceived. How much the practice of tough love stands in stark contrast to what experts now suggest for struggling adolescents. What a false promise these fallible, vulnerable, and terrified human beings were sold.

CHAPTER XIII

Alyssa

By the winter of 2011, the dream Alyssa had so long been chasing materialized. Graduation was upon her, meaning that she was finally free to leave Ponca Pines.

In the lead-up to the ceremony, the school leaned heavily into sacrament. The girls painted concrete stepping-stones, a ritual at Ponca Pines that had them mixing vibrant shades of pinks, oranges, and yellows to decorate the campus's pathways. They also made scrapbooks of their time together. Pieces of brightly colored construction paper bound together and adorned with stickers, snapshots, and collages. One of the pages included notes from a therapeutic exercise that required the girls to write down what they'd like to give every other girl "permission" to do. Reading over Alissa's scrapbook, I see a message from Alyssa where she gave Alissa permission to see and accept her inner and outer beauty. Alissa had pasted it alongside a letter from Alyssa that was full of inside jokes. *Never thought I'd be the one writing you the goodbye note…Unless it meant I was about to jump out my window. Hardy har har.*

While all graduations are symbolic, at therapeutic boarding school, they're more metaphorical. They occur not when students are done with their education—though they'll often have completed their GEDs by then—but when a group of students has completed enough levels of the program and is deemed fit to go home. When it was time for Alyssa's graduation, Elissa, Alissa, and Allie had also climbed high enough through the program's ranks. And though it was a nontraditional graduation, the administration prepared for the ceremony with the same zeal as any other school. A choice likely made more to impress students' parents, a way to maintain the merry veneer they'd sold them on, than to actually celebrate the girls.

Still, the girls allowed themselves to be swept up in the pageantry. They wore matching shiny black lamé caps and gowns but underneath were able to dress as they pleased, liberated from their starchy green polos and khakis. It had been so long since Alyssa or any of the girls had gotten gussied up. Photos that I found show Alyssa in a navy striped shirt with a low-hanging pendant. Elissa in jeans and heeled sandals. Alissa's hair flatironed and her signature smudgy black liner.

"Look how cute you are!" Alyssa said to Elissa as the girls greeted one another before posing for the first round of photos of the day.

"Alissa, you too! Your hair looks perfect," she continued.

"Thaaaaank you," Alissa said, flipping her hair in front of her shoulders.

"We ready for this?" Alyssa asked.

"Guess so," Elissa said, gravitating toward the center of the girls' huddle, situating herself front and center in the camera's frame.

My own graduation at Wheeler's auxiliary campus, referred to as "the farm," had all the girls in white dresses and boys in ties bearing the school's colors of purple and gold. My dress was knitted, with three-quarter-length sleeves, and I spent the day absentmindedly futzing with them as I thought about how in just a few months I'd be at Pitzer College, a small liberal arts school in California, worlds away. I'd attended Wheeler for fifteen years, and I anxiously kept trying to imagine a version of myself outside the school I'd so long felt synonymous with.

Thinking over my decade and a half at Wheeler, my mind snaked back to the early years with Elissa. How she used to kick my ass on the monkey bars in kindergarten, the time she slit her eyelid open on a patch of black ice in first grade. Elissa crossed my mind less often by my senior year, now that I was newly content with the friends that I'd made and the indie-leaning, literature-loving identity I'd worked so hard to cultivate. But in the more significant moments—the ones I'd grown up believing Elissa and I would share—she always came creeping back into my consciousness. A few months before graduation, in my senior year creative writing elective, I put the pull she still had on me into words: *Elissa's translucent ghost follows me, I see her, somewhere behind, invisible and veins.*

Ponca Pines' ceremony was held inside, its halls now decorated with metallic Mylar balloons shaped like stars. Representatives from each of the girls' families attended the ceremony. Claire had brought along Mary and her daughters, who posed for photos alongside the girls, climbing all over Elissa, who had taken a liking to them. Elissa's mother, Julie, mingled with everyone, including Louise and Richard.

The ceremony kicked off with a recitation of Dr. Seuss's *Oh, the Places You'll Go!*, followed by a personalized address from Melody to the girls. Then it was time for Melody to pass the baton to Jess, who had been tasked with handing the students their diplomas. Jess stood by two small wooden tables that had framed photo collages of each girl propped on each. They walked up to grab their diplomas, and each girl paused in front of the table for a picture before shaking hands with Jess and smiling out at the crowd.

Taking in the reception, Louise was proud of what Alyssa had accomplished at Ponca Pines. Alyssa had received her GED and enrolled in an online college-level psychology course. But even as Louise tried her best to remain in the present, solely focusing on Alyssa and this good moment, there was only so much she could do to stop her thoughts from drifting into the unknown and what might lie ahead. Louise had recently been diagnosed with breast cancer—the beginning of an arduous battle that required her to undergo surgery, chemotherapy, and radiation.

It had been a long time since Alyssa and Louise had been entirely on good terms. After Louise and Richard's visit to Ponca Pines for Alyssa's birthday, Alyssa barely spoke on their calls. The only actual updates Louise received about Alyssa's life came filtered through Melody, who assured Louise that Alyssa was improving. But Louise wasn't able to witness this supposed progress. She only felt her daughter retreating further from her, deeper behind her walls.

Then Alyssa received the news that seemed to overshadow any of the prior grievances or grudges she'd held toward her mother. After finding out about her mother's diagnosis, a thawing began to permeate their ensuing conversations. Alyssa started engaging with her mother, worrying about her and all that she was going through back in Northbrook.

But her mother's revelation also coincided with the discovery of another piece of distressing news: Elissa and Alissa had been given the clear to go home. While Alyssa was happy for her friends, the idea of being left behind was gutting. Between her desire to be there for her mother, and her desire to no longer be at Ponca Pines, an idea started to coalesce.

"When her friends finished the program, Alyssa began to beg to come home. She said she wanted to be with me as I went through treatment, and she said she didn't want anything to do with Owen anymore. We wanted so badly to believe her and we let her come home," Louise says now.

In the ceremony photos, Alyssa looks genuinely happy. Standing beside Elissa and Alissa, she seems free of the social anxiety that had plagued her throughout her life. She'd been right to bring Alyssa home, Louise thought as she looked at her daughter draped in traditional cap and gown. Melody had let Louise know that it was her belief that drugs weren't really an issue for Alyssa. Even though Alyssa had previously undergone a psychiatric evaluation at Pacific Quest that found she was at a very high risk for addiction, a fact that never fully escaped Louise's mind. In that moment, Louise opted for optimism. To believe in her daughter.

Many parents feel this optimism upon their children's graduation from the Troubled Teen Industry. While there isn't much research about the effects of the industry, there's one study that administrators often like to share with parents. A study called "Residential Outcomes: Report of Findings from a Multi-Center Study of Youth Outcomes in Private Residential Treatment," the first in-depth examination of the effects of private residential treatment. Researchers sampled nearly one thousand adolescents—most of whom, like Alyssa, were white and from middle- to upper-class socioeconomic backgrounds—and found that there was a significant reduction in problems from the time students first enrolled in the program to when they graduated. The conclusion was that private residential treatments are largely successful in the rehabilitation of their students.[1]

But the industry doesn't go out of its way to alert parents that the study was funded by the Aspen Education Group, an organization that owns and operates a series of different wilderness programs, residential therapeutic boarding schools, and weight loss clinics, as a recruitment tool. That Aspen also guided the research, while neglecting to provide a control group to be studied counter to its some one thousand participants, rendered the study both biased and inconclusive.

These findings also exist in opposition to the many graduates I encounter, who immediately went back to drinking, drugging, or whatever vices got them sent away in the first place. Oftentimes in a more extreme capacity than what had come before. Even the lucky ones, who have come away rehabilitated, still stress the propensity of relapse, many sharing with me some version of the same refrain: *When you've been in the Troubled Teen Industry, you don't go to weddings or birthday parties. Just funerals.*

At the time, Louise would have had no reason to question the industry's promises. She idled around the rec room alongside Richard, making small talk with the other parents about their girls' big day as Alyssa, Alissa, and Elissa hung in a corner, making plans for a reunion over the summer. Alyssa was set to return to Northbrook to care for her mother while the other girls had been accepted at various colleges. Elissa would attend Susquehanna University in Pennsylvania. Alissa was going one state over to attend Iowa Western Community College. The Troubled Teen Industry had made good on their pledge. The girls were going to school, accepting life's responsibilities, reassuming their position on the socially acceptable path that had once stretched in front of them.

"If you don't come to Providence this summer I'll legitimately kill you," Elissa said to Alyssa and Alissa.

"I'm coming! For real," Alissa said.

The thought of Providence anchored them. The oath that they'd reconvene before heading off in different directions, whether starting over or moving on, gave some meaning and a bittersweet ending to their time at Ponca Pines. As excited as Alyssa was by the prospect of leaving—of finally, successfully escaping—it had been over two years since she had been a participant in the real world and her social anxiety was creeping into the seams of her plans. It seemed like a lifetime ago that she'd had any agency over anything, from what she wore to how she spent her days. Ponca Pines had taught her how to survive within its delicate ecosystem but neglected to prepare her for the outside world. One where temptation lurks and there isn't always someone standing guard to stop her from succumbing to vices she'd been told to avoid.

"A toast?" Elissa offered, raising her glass of Diet Coke. "Save our souls."

"Save our fucking souls," said Alyssa.

"Hear, hear."

Save our souls. The more I grieved, the more the expression maddened me. It was further evidence that Elissa had a greater connection with these two women than the one she had with me. *None of our inside jokes were tattooed on each other's bodies,* I couldn't help but think. Maybe our friendship wasn't the same for her. *Would Elissa have been this devastated if I'd been the one who died?* I tried not to wonder.

The phrase became a catchall for all my mixed-up, misplaced anger toward Alyssa and Alissa. For being the friends who had gotten those last years with her, for having lived through something with her so profound that I lacked the knowledge to understand it. But the phrase was also my tipping point. Getting so under my skin that it inspired me to go back and try to uncover why it was meaningful enough for them to have it etched on their flesh, along with the other mysteries of their time together at Ponca Pines.

CHAPTER XIV

Elissa

The first time I saw Elissa again was at a hookah bar the spring after her graduation from Ponca Pines. We'd planned to meet up and I'd brought along my new best friend, Gretchen, whom I'd grown close to my junior year at Wheeler. Unlike Elissa, Gretchen was an emotionally sturdy friend, serious about her desire to study medicine in college, but just as serious about her desire to party. My equal in our ability to juggle academics with revelry.

It had been more than two years since I'd seen Elissa, and though I'd been eager to reconnect with her, I was also apprehensive about the reunion. I was a different person than when I'd seen Elissa last—my own heterogeneous individual and not her symbiotic sidekick—but I still worried about how quickly I could become absorbed by her vortex. I sensed I could forgo my hard-won autonomy to become Elissa's "person" again. So I had Gretchen join us, to remind myself who I'd become, as well as to show Elissa how much I'd grown. When Elissa scooted up to our table, the buffer seemed pointless. There was no match for Elissa's magnetism.

At first, we made small talk. Passing the long, rubber pipe of the hookah back and forth among the three of us. Taking milky pulls of menthol-laced smoke, Elissa deflected any questions I asked about her time at Spring Ridge. (Failing to even mention that she'd actually ended up graduating from Ponca Pines. A fact I wouldn't learn until years later.) Instead, she showed me her *Save our souls* tattoo for the first time and plied me with questions about life at Wheeler. It all felt oddly performative. Like I was doing my best to play the part of a cool girl, and in turn, she was trying to act like a normal high school grad. I fidgeted nervously with the hookah, taking extra hits, ashamed of how hard I was trying.

"Seriously, Sami?" Elissa asked as I spread my bareMinerals lip gloss tube over my lips.

"What?" I asked.

"You still don't know how to do it right," she teased.

There were two things Elissa spent our childhood making fun of me for: how embarrassed I was of my own feet and that I lacked the coordination to properly rub in my lip gloss. Awkwardly pressing my lips together instead of moving them from side to side.

"You're such a bitch."

"You never change, Palm."

The casual exchange of our past inside jokes unraveled the false airs I'd attempted to project. I felt free to express how much I'd missed her, and to actually believe her when she said the same about me. But like always, Elissa didn't have long. Some boy named Jeremy was waiting for her. I remembered him. She'd had a fling with him before she was sent away, back when he had baby pink braces and wore polo shirts that matched the metal in his mouth. We jointly recounted to Gretchen the time they'd fooled around and he ejaculated in her eye. A mishap that we used to laugh about for hours on end. It startled me how vividly I remembered each and every detail, as if it had been my own eye. It also reminded me why I'd allowed myself to remain in Elissa's storm for so long. Being in her orbit made everything more electric. Any night could end up the best night ever; any bad experience could make for the best story of all time. She was just really fucking fun to be around.

When the coals stopped burning, and the shisha had run out, Gretchen offered to drive Elissa to meet Jeremy. The two of them had hit it off—bonding over their ability to blow O's, a skill I was never able to master—and on the drive we exchanged Twitter handles and made plans to go to a party together over the weekend. Then we pulled over on the street Jeremy had designated. Elissa got out and walked confidently into the night.

"See you soon?" Elissa shouted through the dark.

"Definitely," I said.

"Love you."

"Love you too."

That night in bed, I thought little about how Elissa's night might've ended. The next morning, I felt proud for not worrying about it. It was progress: I'd allowed myself to spend time in Elissa's orbit and succeeded in extracting myself from it before chaos hit.

Then my mother came knocking on my door, letting me know that Elissa's mom was here to see me. My bedroom was above our garage and had lilac-painted, slanted walls that jutted out and caved in at different points of the ceiling. Depending on where they stood, even the shortest of my friends would hit their head. But Julie came right in, hovering above my bed in a worried trance.

"Elissa's not here?" Julie asked.

"No? Did she say she was?" I responded.

"She said she was sleeping here. When's the last time you saw her?"

"Umm, she met up with other people after the hookah bar."

"Typical, typical, typical."

"I'm sorry? I didn't realize—"

"It's fine. Sorry to have bothered you."

She turned to leave as quickly as she came. I watched her from my window heading back to her car, continuing her hunt for Elissa. I looked at my BlackBerry, contemplating whether to shoot Elissa a warning text that Julie was on the warpath. In just one night, we'd all fallen back into our old selves. Julie, the frenzied and fearful mother. Elissa, the reckless, rash daughter. Me, the custodial best friend. But I chose not to send the text, actively fighting the stentorian sound in my head shouting out to help her. Instead, I made plans to go out for bagels with Gretchen and our other friends to remind myself that I had a full, rich life outside of Elissa. That she could just be my friend, not my responsibility.

In the weeks that followed, Elissa and I kept chatting. She'd tag me in nostalgic tweets like, *where my wheeler bitches* and *palm/ivy*, and send me equally sentimental messages about our middle school mischief. It felt good to be close again, while still maintaining a careful distance. That was until she started spending more time with another former friend of ours. Chloe went to our rival school, and when we'd first gotten to know her, she was an alt girl. A thin brunette who loved *Lords of Dogtown*, emo music, and skulls. By the time Elissa came back to Providence, Chloe had blossomed, becoming even thinner, and blond. She was now a bona fide popular girl, running with a group that referred to themselves as the "sicko squad."

Elissa and Chloe took to each other with a vengeance, which I watched play out in the tweets they exchanged and the Facebook photos they tagged each other in. It made me feel like the time Elissa and I had gotten into a fight in middle school and she bumped me from her MySpace Top 8. As if I'd been vacated from that best friend spot.

Elissa had gotten a job as a cashier at a greasy spoon called Better Burger Company, but whenever she wasn't at work, she was with Chloe. There was so much Elissa had missed out on during her time away, and Chloe played tutor, bringing her up to speed. She introduced Elissa to Nicki Minaj, and *Pink Friday* became the soundtrack of their summer. Chloe showed her Elissa on Tumblr, the site they'd spend afternoons poring over, looking for new tattoo inspiration. And it was Chloe who inspired Elissa to ditch the straitlaced clothing she'd taken to wearing at Ponca Pines. The two of them started to match: denim booty shorts and crop tops.

Elissa also got to know the other members of the sicko squad: two equally skeletal, raven-haired girls named Sadie and Violet. While Elissa and I had cosplayed Paris and Nicole, the sicko squad had actually become those women incarnate. Together they were the physical embodiment of Lindsay, Britney, and Paris's 2006 *New York Post* cover that has become synonymous with early aughts revelry: an image of the three drunkenly crammed together in a car, plastered over with the headline "Bimbo Summit."

All three girls were good, genuine friends to Elissa, but came equipped with their own demons. They'd also become infamous in Providence. For their taut bodies, free-spirited natures, and predilection for coke. Despite Elissa's proximity, she hesitated to participate in the drugs, even when it was explained to her that they were meant only to enhance their good times, nothing more. But the lesson of Ponca Pines was still rattling around inside her. "I feel like I can't even snort things because of my nose job," Elissa said to Chloe one day, hanging out in her brown Honda CR-V.

The two had been driving aimlessly around Providence until they pulled over at "urban beach"—the parking lot behind the BYOB Japanese restaurant where we'd all go to pregame before parties—to kill more time.

"I got my nose done, too. It's totally fine," Chloe reminded her.
"Really?"
"Yup."
"Fuck it then. Lemme try."

While I wouldn't try coke until college, it was already omnipresent at our parties in my senior year. Friends of mine, huddling together in bathrooms, alternating railing lines. My peers fit the exact mold of a teenage cocaine user. Matching the depictions I coveted onscreen—Sarah Michelle Gellar's Kathryn in *Cruel Intentions*, subtly taking bumps from the coke she kept in her rosary; consummate bad girl Marissa Cooper, turning to the drug in the later seasons of *The O.C.*—as well as the profile put forth by a 2017 study from Arizona State University.[1] Researchers examined two groups of students in affluent New England communities and found that despite being popular and performing well in school, they were far more likely to use cocaine as well as other drugs than national norms. I, too, have found this to be true. In talking to the friends I've made as an adult—who grew up in less affluent communities, farther away from the coasts—I've learned coke wasn't common among their peers. But in my friend group, it was the next logical step after weed and alcohol. A country club drug, the vice of the yuppies before us.

Elissa's drug use had become so casual when I met up with her again that I nearly failed to register it. It was now summer, and Elissa had invited me out to dinner with her and the sicko squad. I accepted: Having stalked the photos they'd been posting from the various house parties they'd been attending, I couldn't stop myself from wanting to get in on the action.

The night of the dinner, Chloe picked me up at my house. Lil Wayne had just dropped the *Sorry 4 the Wait* mixtape and we blasted it on the drive, playing his riff on Kreayshawn's "Gucci Gucci" on repeat. *One big room, full of bad bitches*, we sang out in unison. The wail of overeager white girls, attempting to rap along with the beat, Elissa sitting shotgun and wiggling around in the seat. Trying to dance but mostly just posing, throwing up peace signs and sticking her tongue out at no one and everyone.

The restaurant was nearly empty when we arrived. We'd selected an unpopular Chinese banquet hall, one with so few patrons that it gave off the appearance of a Bond villain lair. The roof boasted an atrium, with a small garden full of oversized shrubs resting in the center of the room, beneath the windowed ceiling. Sitting down, we ordered family style. A pupu platter, large scorpion bowl, and various appetizers for the table. I'd known every member of the sicko squad in various capacities—Providence being small, the private school circuit even smaller—but with their new-found reputations, I'd taken to viewing them as local celebrities. Even though underneath their sicko personas, they were just my peers dressed in bodycon and push-up bras. A truth that became more apparent as they spoke.

"Auggie's blowing up my phone," Chloe said.

"Ben's hitting me up, too," Elissa said.

"How cute would it be if we actually dated best friends?"

"Chloe the Baddest and E Nasty Swag, besties *with* best bros."

"What about Davey?" Violet asked.

"He's still in the picture," Elissa responded.

"That's what I like to hear, E Money," Sadie said.

"Be right back," Elissa said, excusing herself to head to the bathroom. They kept chatting, unable to temper their excitement over the parties they had lined up for the night, the boys they were talking to, the gossip they'd heard. Auggie, one of Providence's local drug dealers and Chloe's latest paramour, was having a kickback later on. Sadie complained about her boyfriend, whom she'd been dating on and off again since middle school. And Violet was reading off her texts from Nick, the party boy she was seeing who had briefly been sent to a wilderness program for his drinking. I listened intently, nodding along, wondering why Elissa was taking so long to come back.

"You guys miss me?" Elissa asked upon her return.

"Always," Chloe said.

"Did you finish that bag?" Violet asked.

"No... Sharing is caring!"

"Thanks, boo."

Elissa sat back down, slipping a miniature coke baggie into Violet's hands before reclaiming her scorpion bowl straw and taking a large gulp. I knew it was hypocritical of me to be bothered that Elissa was doing coke—I had every intention of trying it sometime in the near future—but I was too overcome by a series of erratic emotions. Mad, judgmental, scared, and lame all at once. Mostly I was still resentful of the dynamic so deeply embedded in my and Elissa's friendship that I couldn't let her do a line of coke without worrying about her. An overwhelming and overpowering feeling that I couldn't quite grasp until I started to attend Al-Anon. Not understanding where the urge to fix Elissa came from, or why that desire had such power over me.

Once the egg rolls, spare ribs, and crab rangoon had been depleted, we piled back into the car with another round of Weezy's crackling rasp. They invited me to come with them to Auggie's, but I opted to go home out of self-preservation. Afraid that if I spent more time with Elissa, I'd spin out even further.

My mom, her boyfriend, and my sister were out of town, leaving me with the house to myself for the summer. Gretchen slept over most nights, along with a slew of our other friends who were too drunk to drive home. But that night, Gretchen and I hung out alone in my backyard, ripping hits from the acrylic bong we'd gone in on together while I shared the highlights from dinner.

Careful not to mention the anxiety I'd felt at Elissa's drug use out of fear that I'd come across like a narc. And deep down because I was far too embarrassed by how quickly I'd gone back to those subservient tendencies I'd spent so much time trying to shed.

Why is Elissa trying to blow up her life? I wondered later on that evening. It enraged me that this seemed like the only way she knew how to live. Being the good-time girl was the role she'd always wanted to inhabit, and I felt naive for thinking this time would be any different. But what I didn't understand then was that in Ponca Pines' attempt to reform her, they had only created a binary. A world where she could either be the perfect young woman that they wanted her to be or the troubled teen she'd come to them as. When Elissa chose the latter, she reverted back to her hard-partying, risk-prone former self. A choice that made me summon the courage to do something I hadn't been able to do in the past: take a step back from Elissa.

Not long after, I looked down at my phone one day to see a flurry of texts from Elissa. We texted a lot throughout the summer, usually inviting each other to parties that one of us would inevitably flake on—her too caught up in the sicko squad; me trying to keep that healthy distance—but these messages were different. It was clear she was seeking actual commitment. And while I declined this invitation, not accepting is a regret that I've returned to again and again on this journey.

In the text, Elissa had invited me to go see a Backstreet Boys concert with her and a girl who at the time I'd never heard her mention before. One of her best friends from boarding school, Alissa.

———

Alissa's visit to Providence went by in a blur of selfies. Having spent the entirety of their friendship in isolation at Ponca Pines, without cell phones, their friendship didn't have much of a digital footprint. Aside from a few photos from their school outings—a trip to a bowling alley, a dinner at a restaurant in Omaha—as well as images from graduation, there was nothing to memorialize what they meant to each other. But during Alissa's Providence trip, Elissa made sure to rectify that. They took mirror selfies, crouched on the floor of Elissa's bedroom, middle fingers in the air. They snapped shots of themselves on the bow of Elissa's family's boat, cozied up and crusty from the salt water. And they posed for photos in Elissa's front yard, the place where we took the best photos in the heyday of our times together. Later, after Alissa had also passed away, I'd revisit these photos. Staring at this girl who had begun to feel all too familiar to me, despite never having met her at all.

In the months after Ponca Pines, Elissa didn't say much to me about her experience there. Not to me, Chloe, or any of her other friends. When any of us would ask her about it outright, she'd avoid answering the question, claiming she preferred to live in the present. But Alissa's visit was an opportunity to delve into it all. Alissa held no shame about what she'd been through, having spoken openly to her home friends and family about her experiences. Lying around Elissa's now fluorescent lime-green bedroom, they talked about some of the happier times there.

"Oh my god, do you remember picture day?" Alissa asked.

"When you, like, couldn't get yourself to smile!" Elissa said.

"You were doing the craziest shit."

"I mean, I needed to get you to smile!"

Elissa invited another childhood friend of ours, Molly, to the concert with them when I declined. The Backstreet Boys were playing at Mohegan Sun, a casino in Connecticut about an hour from Providence. Julie had remarried, and her husband's son, Mike, was working security at the casino. Mike was a tatted-up muscle head whom Elissa had taken to, and in turn, he'd scored her free tickets to the show. Her brother Seth, forever her most loyal companion, drove the girls, taking the '90s throwback jams in alongside them.

Elissa and Alissa wore matching gray outfits for the concert. Alissa in an empire waist dress that was bejeweled around the scooped neckline and Elissa in a gray crop top that had fringe jutting out on the bottom. They took loads of photos. Hanging on each other in front of the slot machines, sitting pretty in the stands. Then the music came on, and the two danced as they scream-sang the lyrics, Elissa replicating her peace-sign-laden movements while Alissa shook her hips. It had been years since Elissa had gone to a concert, so long since either one of them had been able to cut loose. It didn't matter that the band was past their prime, or that the girls much preferred rap to pop. They were giddy to just be together in such an environment like other teenage girls, at last.

After Alissa went back to Nebraska, she shared the photos in her own Facebook album dedicated to the trip. When I got around to stalking them, it was that giddiness I registered first. How at ease they looked in each other's company, utterly delighted to be together. Alissa would repost the photos often in the ensuing years. For Elissa's birthday; on the anniversary of her death. Returning to them, both then and now, I find myself searching for some hidden meaning. Some sign that would help make sense of how they both could possibly be gone. But all I ever see is a portrait of true friendship. Two vital, vibrant teenage girls.

CHAPTER XV

Elissa

Elissa had developed a reputation for passing out at parties. While she'd struggled to find her footing at Susquehanna University—unsure of what to focus her studies on, or how to focus on studying—she'd made a name for herself on the party scene. Early on she befriended the guys who lived in the hockey house and the lacrosse house, as well as the spot that had been dubbed "the manor." And while their parties were flooded with freshman girls, Elissa stood out from the pack. She was at ease among the debauchery: sniffing out the supply of liquor, casually asking around for coke. She would dance in various corners of the houses' basements littered with beer and junk. Posters that featured the American flag, signs that read *no smoking* and begged to be disobeyed. Hanging around until the wee hours of the morning, drinking until the booze ran dry. Keeping the night going until her barely-one-hundred-pound body gave out, crashing on the closest soft surface.

More often than not, Elissa could be found with Leah, the curly-haired stoner girl who lived down the hall from her. They'd first encountered each other during a welcome meeting for their dorm, when Elissa raised her hand to confess that she'd spaced out and had failed to retain anything from the presentation. Elissa intimidated Leah. Her straight talking, that disregard for social convention. But as much as Leah found these traits daunting, they also drew her to Elissa. The same push-pull I'd been grappling with all summer long, and all the years before it. Elissa also found comfort in Leah. Spending her days curled up in the purple butterfly chair Leah kept in the dorm room, her new refuge. As much as ancillary characters like Leah and I were moths to Elissa's flame, she was also drawn to us. We gave her a steadying presence, a necessary tonic to her bedlam. And Leah was more than happy to oblige.

I'd seen Elissa one last time before I left for college, having stopped in at Better Burger Company for a Nutella milkshake and to give her a farewell hug. We texted irregularly during my first semester—like the time she reached out, asking about a guy she used to hook up with who also attended Pitzer—but outside of that, our interactions primarily consisted of liking the Facebook photos we both posted to show the world just how much fun we were having in college.

Most of my photos were with Lena, the hipster Jewish girl from the Valley who was in both my introduction to anthropology and film studies courses. Lena was beautiful: blond and bespectacled, frequently drawing comparisons to Brigitte Bardot or Jane Birkin in *La Piscine*. Her modelesque looks made her a celebrity among our school's small, thousand-person student body, and my proximity to her made me a minor one. My first few weeks at school were difficult. Plagued with homesickness, regret for going so far away, fear that I'd end up transferring. Making friends with Lena felt exciting, especially the attention I received by association. We traded shoes—my floral Dr. Martens for her studded combat boots—and I adopted her signature makeup look: one slick, skinny streak of black liquid eyeliner.

Leah was also enjoying the perks of her friendship with Elissa. VIP entrance to all the parties, the embrace of the school's fast crowd, a budding reputation as one of her grade's cool girls. All of which empowered her to party harder, attempting to keep up with Elissa. It's a time she still looks back on fondly when we reconnect. Leah and I first met the summer after we graduated from college, when we both attended the Columbia Publishing Course. That summer, I failed to point out the connection to Leah, who hadn't made it herself. Three years into my grief, but still far too deep in the trenches to be able to make small talk about our mutual friend between lectures on book publishing. Ducking from her in the lunchroom; afraid she'd figure it out. And when we finally do speak of Elissa, six years after that summer, I can't shake how mortified I feel about my former self. Yet sad, too. That I'd been so hellbent on hiding and holding on to my version of Elissa, instead of welcoming the chance to learn more about her mysterious last months. Like the story Leah tells me now, of when her high school boyfriend, Jonah, came to party with them for the weekend.

Arriving at Susquehanna, Jonah revealed a surprise he'd brought along for the weekend: Oxy. Elissa had tried the drug before, once or twice with the sicko squad, who had begun taking it intermittently, and were eager to do it again. At that point, I didn't know the people I grew up with were doing Oxy. Having no idea that Elissa, the sicko squad, or any of our mutual friends had tried it. It wasn't like coke—where people were doing it out in the open, casually offering lines to the other partygoers—Oxy was a more private, personal pastime. But, as I'd learn the following year, opioids were all over Providence. My eyes just weren't open to them yet.

The opioid epidemic began in the mid-'90s, when doctors started overprescribing opioids. But these doctors weren't pushing opioids on just anyone. Studies show that the doctors were less likely to prescribe opioids to minorities—falsely believing that minority patients would be more likely to misuse or sell the drugs—instead, primarily prescribing them to white Americans. This led to a surplus of opioids in the suburbs, places like Providence, where there were so many of the drugs lying around they began to proliferate, with patients gifting excess pills to their friends, teens stealing them from the medicine cabinet, some even selling them on the black market. By 2011, oxycodone use had increased over fivefold. Especially among my peers, who fell squarely into the demographic most frequently abusing opioids: young adults ages eighteen to twenty-five.

After agreeing to try Jonah's Oxy, Elissa and Leah snuck off to Deg—the hub where the dining hall, a Starbucks, the student-run coffee shop, and a small food court were all held—to grab the necessary wares. The method they'd chosen for ingestion was smoking, making tinfoil an essential part of the operation. Entering Deg, they scanned the building's salad bar, deli, and hot food bar, looking for the to-go station. They located tinfoil amid the containers, plastic utensils, and deli papers and smuggled sheets of foil back to the dorm.

Jonah carefully instructed the girls on the intricacies of smoking it. First ripping the tinfoil into small slits. Then handing Leah a straw, directing her to place one tip in her mouth, with the other hovering just above the single Oxy he'd placed on the foil. When Leah brought a lighter to the other side of the slit, the pill instantly began to shift from the force of the flame. As it burned, the Oxy transformed from its traditional white to a light, grubby yellow. The foil also grew black and chalky in spots, the heat having begun to whittle away at the aluminum. All the while Leah kept inhaling the fumes.

"Did I do it right?" Leah asked Jonah.

"For sure, for sure," he said.

"Okay! Me next," Elissa said.

After Leah and Elissa both had their turns, they cuddled up in Leah's bed while Jonah sat at the desk, looking up at them. While I've never taken OxyContin—not having swallowed, snorted, smoked, or shot any form of opiates—a friend once described the experience in a way that's always stuck with me. She told me that it felt like a great unclenching. One hit of Oxy and suddenly she stopped curling her toes, grinding her teeth, and stiffening her shoulders. Every limb had been loosened, every ounce of tension set free. And Elissa and Leah sat on the bed, their heads whirling around, propelled by their incessant, unrelenting laughter.

"Want some more?" Jonah asked.

"Yeah. Definitelyyyyy," Elissa said.

"Coming on up!" Jonah said, reaching back into the pill bottle, grabbing what was left of his stash. As the girls failed to steady themselves, still too wobbly from all the giggling, Jonah popped a pill into each of their mouths, with the rest of the evening carrying on in the same manner: laughter, refueling, then more laughter.

Coming down from the high, Leah determined that she'd enjoyed the experience. How out of her body she'd felt, how silly everything had seemed. But in the days that followed she didn't think much more of it, while all Elissa could think about was how much she wanted to do Oxy again. Starting to ask around for it at parties, joking that she'd make a cute lady Oxy dealer. That was the rub of being friends with Elissa. To be in her orbit was to always be renegotiating how much you were willing to stretch your limitations, what you were willing to do to keep up.

Leah underwent some form of this negotiation each time they went out. Because no matter how late she'd stay at the party, Elissa would always want to stay longer, remaining at the party for so long that Leah had no choice but to leave her behind. At first, Leah was hesitant about letting Elissa fend for herself. But after it happened over and over again, she grew to trust that Elissa would be okay. There was always someone coming to Elissa's rescue. Carrying her home, or back to their bed, where they'd wait for her to rise from her blackout. Sometimes rewarding their heroism with sex.

By sophomore year, I was also partying a lot. I'd drink gin and tonics to kick things off, chasing them with a line of Molly, and doing coke throughout the night to keep myself leveled out. The combination made me feel confident, in control. All those things that I hadn't felt when I first arrived at Pitzer. Sometimes my partying led to nights like Elissa's—where a classmate found me passed out in the bushes, covered in soap from the evening's "foam party"—and to others when I made it home unscathed. Similar to Elissa, I was riding high on invincibility. It was fueled by the fact that I didn't fear losing my scholarship or wasting student loans on partying. I'd grown up on *The Rules of Attraction* and *St. Elmo's Fire*; this was just part of it, I thought.

But what Elissa was experiencing wasn't some over-romanticism of movies. She had gone from being watched as she ate, studied, and sometimes even slept, to total freedom. And in all this policing, she'd been given no preparation for life outside Ponca Pines. Not for how to pick a major or exercise caution when it came to partying. Unlike Leah and me, Elissa didn't have an off switch. While Thursday through Saturday were reserved for blacking out, I spent the other days of the week maintaining my grade point average. Writing ethnographies for my anthropology classes, watching golden-age cinema for my film lectures. Leah spent her weekdays hitting the library, getting ahead on work. And on those nights Elissa would simply seek out someone else to party with. Taking a night off wasn't an option.

Usually, the person who would fill in for Leah was Luke, the six-foot-eight, fifth-year senior Elissa was meant to be "exclusive" with. While Elissa was also regularly seeing two other guys—and often hooking up with those random men who came to her rescue on the party circuit—Luke was the favorite on her roster. They'd spend hours on end hanging around his dorm room. Sometimes doing coke, others listening to Miguel albums.

On one of the evenings that Elissa was off with Luke, Leah decided to hang behind and have a chiller night with some of her other friends. There were many popular smoke spots on campus, and the baseball complex was one of them. It was the off-season, and Leah and the others had posted up in the stadium, smoking a joint and kicking back. Though Leah enjoyed the drugs she and Elissa had tried throughout the semester—the Oxy with Jonah, Molly on another night—weed was always her favorite. And in between taking long, throaty hits of her drug of choice, Leah looked down at her cell phone to find a text from Elissa bearing one singular message, *SOS*.

The text startled her. So many of Leah's nights had consisted of Elissa convincing her that she was totally fine. That Leah shouldn't worry about her, she could handle herself. For Elissa to be seeking help was alarming. I'd experienced this so many years before when Elissa had called me saying that the razor blade had gone too deep. An innate, unwavering desire to be there for Elissa—to talk her through cleaning up the blood, to save her from whatever situation she'd found herself in—but also a quiet fear of whatever havoc Elissa had brought upon herself. As Leah looked back at the text, any fear she might've felt was subsumed by her need to help. She gathered up her belongings, politely excused herself from the smoke sesh, and made her way across campus, straight to Luke's dorm room.

"Hello?" Leah said, knocking on Luke's door.

"Hey, Leah. What are you doing here?" Luke asked.

"Elissa texted me. She here?"

"Yeah, she's sleeping."

Luke returned to his desk, where he and his roommate were huddled together, preoccupied with something on his computer. He was used to seeing Elissa passed out and was unbothered as she lay still under his sheets. Leah walked closer to the bed and Elissa stirred, revealing herself to be entirely naked. Her mascara and eyeshadow had blurred together, now resting under her lower eyelids, bleeding down past her bags. The lower half of her mouth slightly ajar, open just enough to allow for the heavy breathing of a deep, drunken sleep.

"Elissa, are you okay?" Leah asked, pushing on her shoulder.

"Elissa?" Leah repeated, when all Elissa responded with was garbled half words.

Leah looked around for Elissa's clothes, finding them scattered on the ground. She quickly collected them, throwing them on the bed. Trying to rouse Elissa awake.

"C'mon, Elissa. We're gonna head home now," Leah said.

"I'm good," Elissa said finally.

"No, no, it's time to leave," Leah responded.

"I'm fiiiiiiiine," Elissa said.

"Okay, then," Leah said, leaving Elissa exactly the way she'd found her.

While Leah was apprehensive about leaving, she felt as if she had no other choice. Elissa had become defiant, entirely resistant to any of Leah's help or the belief that she needed help in the first place. Vulnerability didn't come easily to Elissa. She'd spent so much time in therapeutic boarding school, in the hot seat, cultivating a veneer of toughness. Never letting on about any internal strife or physical anguish. And while she'd occasionally crack—once crying in front of Leah about how lost she felt in life, another time confiding in her that she had no idea what to do with her future—she'd quickly compose herself, putting back on her mask of being the good-time girl and laughing off the idea that the situation was actually an SOS or making fun of her sudden outburst of emotions. Asserting that everything was *fine*.

It's my belief that this façade was Elissa's trauma response. While being in the Troubled Teen Industry hasn't technically been classified as a form of trauma, the experience meets many of the prerequisites. Research out of the National Institutes of Health defines *trauma* as "experiences that cause intense physical and psychological stress reactions."[1] Many of the industry's practices are likely to perpetuate such stress reactions. Be it the restraining, placing in solitary confinement, or drugging that many of Elissa's peers experienced, or the verbal abuse Elissa herself lived through. Being attacked by her peers while in the hot seat, time and time again, the aftershocks of the exercise catching up to her, no matter how hard she tried to defy its effects.

Like I had for many years, Leah had no choice but to go along with it. Being there for Elissa in the moment, then pretending nothing had happened when the moment passed. A few days later, still acting like nothing had happened in Luke's room, Elissa invited Leah to go with her off campus. Susquehanna Valley Mall was just a quick drive and Elissa had been itching to buy new lingerie. The mall was short on options for intimates. There was a Hobby Lobby, a Kay Jewelers, a Bath & Body Works, and other shops. Elissa settled on Spencer's, navigating through its dim-lit aisles full of knock-off CBGB T-shirts, lava lamps, and drinking-inspired board games. The lingerie ran the gamut of fantasies. Schoolgirl looks, naughty nurse slip sets, lace kimono robes. The girls examined them all, with Elissa ultimately landing on something more traditional, less of a costume.

Alongside the mall's chain shops, there was a small, sketchy-seeming piercing parlor. She'd been talking about getting her tongue pierced for a while, and when she happened upon the parlor, it felt like kismet. She still had a few days before fall break, ample time for her tongue to heal just enough so she could try to hide it from her mom.

"I can't stop drooling," Elissa said as she held her tongue out, clamped but still awaiting the needle.

"Happens to everyone," said the piercer.

"Ahh! I don't know if I can watch," Leah said.

"Okay, deep breath. You ready?" the piercer asked.

"Yup," Elissa said, more concerned with her drooling than anything else.

Leah loved sharing these moments with Elissa. Being party to her impulsivity, the adrenaline rush that was her life. In the lead-up to fall break, they continued to spend the majority of their free time together. Elissa was feeling run-down and had been going out less. She'd made a ton of plans for the break—the sicko squad was coming home, as was I, and we'd been texting about getting together—so she spent her last few days on campus resting up, trying to break her slight fever. Leah played nurse, bringing her Gatorade, keeping her company as she lay in bed.

"I gave the health center a call," Leah said on one of her visits.

"Why?" Elissa asked.

"Because you feel like shit so you should probably go?"

"No, no. I'm fine."

"I'll go with you!"

"I'm all good."

Leah left and Elissa fired up a tweet that made me laugh when I read it while scrolling through my timeline. *When I'm sick and I need my mom I pretend that I don't have a tattoo, tongue piercing or belly button ring @psychogrlprblem,* she wrote.

CHAPTER XVI

Alissa

When Alissa found out that Elissa was sick, she was both devastated and hopeful. Keeping Elissa in her prayers, trying to will Elissa to recover through the sheer power of her thoughts. But from the second that I heard Elissa was sick I felt, in my bones, that she wouldn't make it. I was overcome with this instinctual grief. Like this nameless *thing* I'd subconsciously feared my whole life had just happened. The trouble was finally, fully here.

Alissa was in her first semester at Iowa Western Community College when she got the news. While school hadn't been going well for Alissa—her grades were poor enough that her mother would pull her out a few months later—there was one silver lining. She was in her first-ever relationship, with an upperclassman named Anthony. Anthony wasn't exactly what Alissa pictured for her first boyfriend. He was a cheerleader with a husky build and soul patch who went by the nickname Moose. But unlike her best friends Elissa and Alyssa, she hadn't spent her adolescence basking in the adoration of suitors. Her insecurity about her body seemed to repel male attention. She was so paranoid that she'd be perceived as ugly or fat that she didn't even want to be looked at. But Anthony found her beautiful and made sure that she knew it. For a few months, Alissa was genuinely happy.

Then appeared a Facebook post from Seth, Elissa's brother, that would obliterate that happiness:

May 9th, 1993, to October 19th, 2011, 10:35 the world started and ended. I love you, Elissa. Rest in peace.

I first heard Elissa was sick while shopping with my sister at Urban Outfitters. I was home in Providence, walking around the strip of stores that ran parallel to Wheeler, when Gretchen called me to say she'd heard a rumor that Elissa was in the hospital. Growing up, my favorite movie was *The Wizard of Oz*. And the only way I can begin to describe how I felt about Elissa being hospitalized was that I experienced a deteriorating, like when the Wicked Witch started melting, becoming the emotional equivalent of the witch's puddle of black clothing that remained on the floor after she'd dissipated into the ether.

There was about a twenty-four-hour span between the time that I found out Elissa had been hospitalized and when Seth's post went live and declared her dead. But by the time I made it home from Urban Outfitters, I'd already started my mourning process. Throwing my body against my bed and giving myself over to the enormity of my emotions. Breaking down has never been an experience I've felt entirely comfortable with. But alone in my room, it was as if all this hurt I'd been amassing—the anger I felt at Elissa for her recklessness, the fear that had lived inside me over what might happen to her, the loss of my childhood dying alongside her—all came to the surface. The pain I hadn't allowed myself to process, as I was too busy positioning myself as the one who had it all together. The person to lean on, not the one who needed the leaning. But the magnitude of Elissa's death eradicated all my put-together posturing. Suddenly I was doing things that under any other circumstances would've mortified me. Kicking, punching my mattress, screaming into my pillow. They were the screams I'd been holding in for as long as I could remember.

Elissa's official cause of death was encephalitis: an inflammation of the brain. And while her case first presented in a mild fashion—manifesting itself through the flu-like symptoms she was exhibiting at Susquehanna—by the time she entered the hospital the swelling in her brain had grown so severe that she slipped into a coma. In my non-scientifically-inclined mind, I've always pictured what happened as a tidal wave breaking free from a dam. The encephalitis unleashed inside her brain, ravaging its neural pathways, annihilating the various lobes it comprised. This unstoppable force of nature barreling inside her, doing enough damage to render her brain-dead. Leaving her family with the impossible, unfathomable choice of taking her off life support. To surrender to the catastrophe.

Encephalitis can be caused by anything from a mosquito bite to having shingles. Another common precursor is having a bacterial infection, which can result from ingesting drugs through your nasal cavities. A theory that, at times—whether fairly or not—I've harbored about the origin of Elissa's case. But ultimately, they weren't able to determine Elissa's illness's root—leading me to believe that the true cause was inevitability.

For a long time, I couldn't comprehend why I believed that. How come it all felt so preordained? But then a few months later, I had a conversation with my dad's girlfriend, Rebecca, that put my premonition into perspective. For as long as I knew Elissa, her life was defined by her desire to burn the brightest. A hunger to experience it all, despite the consequences, that made her destined to burn fast, and then burn out. Encephalitis was merely the method by which she met her end, not the catalyst.

As is Jewish custom, Elissa's funeral was set for just two days after her death. I spent those forty-eight hours lying in bed, still not having changed out of the oversized gray cashmere sweater I'd been wearing at Urban Outfitters or ceasing to cry. And while I retreated inward, Alissa communed with the Ponca Pines girls. Alyssa, Charlotte, and Halle all shared in Alissa's shock.

Halle and Charlotte lost touch over time, not having seen each other since Ponca Pines or talked much in the years since. Until the three of us decide to get on a three-way phone call, which becomes more of a catch-up between them than a formal interview. With me listening as they fill each other in on motherhood, Charlotte's law school journey, their lives at large. I laugh at their jokes, chime in with the occasional comment, but mostly just let the two of them talk. Gratitude is an emotion I find myself overcome by more often than I would've expected on these calls. The hurt and pain I expected to feel is still there—but the gratitude is just as present, for how much people like Halle and Charlotte have let me into their lives, their willingness to share their stories with me.

On the phone with Charlotte and Halle, they both underscore the same sentiment. That of all the girls, Elissa felt like the one who was going to be okay. That her issues seemed the most benign, making her the friend most poised to rebound from her time at therapeutic boarding school. The likeliest to go on to live a rich, full life.

Though this is a different intuition than the one I maintained, in talking to them I've come to see their point. Elissa's poker face was so powerful—her ability to hold tight to whatever this unknowable thing was that propelled her down her path and sealed her fate—that she really did seem solid. Convincing all of them that she was totally fine, but more importantly, convincing herself. In the immediate aftermath of Elissa's death, as they all made plans to meet up at O'Hare Airport and travel to the funeral together, they discussed their collective shock just as much as their sadness. *How the fuck could this have happened to Elissa?* they would wonder, between consoling one another.

On the day before the funeral, Halle and Alissa drove together to Chicago from Omaha. Charlotte made the trip by herself, coming from her home in Minnesota, while Alyssa was running late, still not having taken the twenty-minute drive from Northbrook to O'Hare.

"Charlotte!" Alissa called out once they'd laid eyes on each other at the security check-in point.

"You guys!" Charlotte said.

"How was the drive?" Halle asked.

"Girl, you have a bubble butt now," Charlotte said.

"What?" Halle asked.

"Like, your ass got fat!" Charlotte replied.

The three of them hadn't been all together since Ponca Pines, and their excitement about reuniting momentarily tempered their grief. Then their conversation turned to the strange phone call Alissa had gotten from Alyssa on the drive. At first, Alissa assumed Alyssa's scattered, evasive energy was just a manifestation of her mourning. The past few days had been so blindsiding, and given Alyssa's habit of shutting down, it was easy to assume that she was just having a hard time articulating all that she was feeling. But as the call went on, Alissa became less sure that grief was the only thing on Alyssa's mind. She kept asking about the flight information, what the trip would entail. Toward the end of the call, Alyssa vaguely mentioned that she might not be able to make it, before walking the comment back.

"She better fucking make it," Charlotte said when Alissa was done with her story.

"Elissa *never* wouldn't have shown up for her," Halle said.

"I think she's gonna make it. She's probably just stressed," Alissa said.

"Fuck it. I'm calling her," Halle said.

On the first few tries, Alyssa let the call go to voicemail. But Halle was relentless, redialing until Alyssa had no choice but to answer.

"Hey," Alyssa said, in the same elusive tone that had unnerved Alissa.

"We're leaving soon. Where are you?" Halle asked.

"I know, I know. I really wanna come."

"Since when are you not coming?"

"I'm just, like, worried."

"About?"

"Like, do you think I can sneak H on the plane?"

"No...I think that's a terrible fucking idea."

Halle and the other girls knew that Owen used, but this was the first time Alyssa confessed to doing so as well. None of the girls were prudes when it came to drugs. Halle and Alissa both had their own relationship with prescription pills; Charlotte had run with drug dealers and drug users alike. While they didn't judge Alyssa for using, they did judge her for missing Elissa's funeral. Clouded by their guilt and grief, they failed to register that Alyssa wasn't being a bad friend; she was just too dependent on the drug to get through the trip without using.

———————

At the funeral, I was too consumed by petty grievances to notice Alissa, Halle, and Charlotte. Just as how humans are unable to comprehend large-scale tragedies, with the brain issuing a psychic numbing as a defense mechanism, my mind had anesthetized itself to the calamity at hand. Sitting in the temple where Elissa and I had both been bat mitzvahed, I couldn't grasp being there without her, let alone for her. Instead, I focused on the things minute enough I could actually grapple with them. Like my seething rage that I hadn't been asked to be a pallbearer.

The sicko squad sat in the front row, in the swath of seats that had been sectioned off, reserved for the pallbearers. I sat with my mom on the same side of the congregation, a few rows behind them, staring at the back of their heads. The wraparound sunglasses that I wore throughout the service obscured my eyes, but if anyone had been able to see through their black tint, they'd see that I spent more time looking over at them than at the proceedings on the pulpit. Their modest black dresses and blow-dried hair burning an impression in my retinas as all my teen insecurities rattled around in my head. Just as I felt when Elissa was off at Ponca Pines and unable to communicate with me, all I could think was how unchosen I felt. As if not being selected as a pallbearer was the ultimate, final confirmation that I didn't matter to Elissa as much as she mattered to me. That she was *my* best friend, but I wasn't hers. Then I'd briefly come to from my internal tantrum and feel like the most grotesque, shameful person in the room. To be so spiteful and so self-absorbed, in this moment of all moments. To think of myself rather than the pain that Elissa's family was experiencing—mourning both Elissa's lost future as well as the years the Troubled Teen Industry had already stolen from them.

Alissa was sitting in one of the synagogue's many other rows, taking it all in. Though she had little familiarity with the Jewish faith, the temple was impressive. Its stained-glass windows with written Hebrew prayers, the dome-like, wooden-thatched ceiling. She was touched by the sheer number of people who had turned up for Elissa. Unlike me—who considered all her other friends a threat, judging their sadness against my own as a measure of closeness—she was in awe of the vast collection of family members, friends, and neighbors. There was a standing-room-only section, along with an overflow of people congregating in the main hall. She joined in when it came time for everyone to sing the kaddish.

"*Yit-ga-dal v'yit-ka-dash sh'mei ra-ba, b'al-ma di-v'ra chi-ru-tei, v'yam-lich mal-chu-tei b'chai-yei-chon uv'yo-mei-chon uv'chai-yei d'chol-beit Yis-ra-eil, ba-a-ga-la u-viz-man ka-riv, v'im'ru: A-mein,*" we all sang in unison.

Alissa fumbled through the prayer. But the kaddish poured right out of me. As kids, Elissa and I made games out of the various chants, songs, and prayers that made up the services. Standing up on our very tiptoes, far past how high we were instructed to go, when singing out *kadosh* during the Kedushah. Speed-singing the shehecheyanu. Or during the kaddish we'd make our voices extra deep, matching the register of the cantor. Singing the kaddish this time, in her honor, was such an overwhelming feeling that it stirred free the grief I'd been working so hard to repress all morning long, trying so hard to hold it together, until I was back in my bed, safe in my gray sweater, alone while I kicked my feet and cried. So I reached into my purse and pulled out the lorazepam I'd brought with me in case of an emergency, dry swallowing it and allowing the promise of its relief to steady me until the funeral concluded.

By the time I finally made it back to my bed—after attending the brief graveside burial that followed the service—the lorazepam had kicked in. Curled up in a ball, I pulled up Elissa's Facebook page on my iPhone, taking in all the new posts, pictures, and prayers that had come in while my phone had been off for the funeral. Scrolling through them, I found myself full of those same feelings I'd had while staring at the sicko squad in the synagogue.

Judging the people who posted on her wall for treating their grief like a pissing contest. Blissfully ignorant to the fact that deep down, even though I'd chosen not to write on her wall, the person who was being competitive about their grief was me.

Alissa headed home to Omaha with Halle after the funeral. At home, she also returned to Elissa's Facebook. It was on the page, not at the temple, that Alissa felt like she could actually reach Elissa. As if the app were an oracle to the afterlife, with Alissa transposing all the things she wished she could tell her right into the textbox.

This is what first made me take notice of Alissa's posts, how unabashed she was in her emotions. Blasting her messages off into the world without any proofreading or obsessing over whether or not her words sounded trite. The opposite of how I would've been, had I opted to post. So desperate to sound clever and original and witty at all times, wielding my ability to do so like armor. Instead, Alissa just brain dumped onto Elissa's profile:

I would do anything in this world to be able to see her one last time. See her beautiful smile and hear her voice one last time.

I used to think everything happens for a reason then when you passed away I stopped believing that. I don't see how there could be a reason for you to pass away.

At first, I thought Alissa was an attention-seeker. An opinion that for years I was embarrassed to have had, but I've since come to give my eighteen-year-old self some grace. I'd spent so much of my time back then burying myself in the emotions of others that I'd neglected to learn about my own. So when that tsunami of hurt kept coming to the surface, I went for anger over acceptance.

Demonizing Alissa, Alyssa, and their *Save our souls* tattoos for being what I thought of as so performative.

Now, over ten years after Elissa's death and three years into writing this book, I'm still nowhere closer to having found evidence of what *Save our souls* actually means. Their classmates, teachers, family members, and friends all remember *Save our souls*, just not its origins, its meaning mystifying them as well. Still, in spite of this, I feel newly confident that I can surmise its significance. *Save our souls* was their catchall: for all the pain and punishment they were put through in the pursuit of being fixed. For their ability to survive rather than surrender.

Save our souls has also come to take on additional significance, one that's mine alone. A symbol of my change in perspective. Finally moving away from all the vitriol and jealousy that ensconced me in the depths of my mourning, I now see the tattoo and their other outpourings of grief as their own attempt to make sense of the senseless. The loss of our best friend.

CHAPTER XVII

Alyssa

Less than a year after Elissa died, Alyssa found herself back in treatment. Alyssa's time as a civilian was as short as it is shrouded in mystery. What I do know is that while Alyssa had moved home with every intention of caring for her mother, Owen's allure became all-consuming, both because of her dependency on him and because of the heroin they were using together.

Similar to how the people in Owen's orbit are unwilling to speak out about him, they're also resistant to opening up about the time Alyssa spent with him back in Northbrook. The months when Owen guided Alyssa on how to bring the syringe to her skin, pushing down at a ninety-degree angle until the heroin went ricocheting through her bloodstream, instantly eradicating the anxiety and unease that for so long had been so unrelenting. As one of the people who used with her wrote to me on Facebook, "I just couldn't find it in myself to even try to give a version of how her life was. She was an amazing girl, unfortunately, we met each other while we were all looking for an escape...She had a few bad years which ended up destroying who she was...Her parents seemed to be trying the best they could, but in reality I think it ended up pushing her further into the void."

For Alyssa's parents, what they believed was best was sending her to another program. Reading journalist David Sheff's 2005 *New York Times Magazine* essay "My Addicted Son," I start to understand just how much this decision must have weighed on Alyssa's parents. How overwhelmed, scared, and lost they must have felt—how desperate they were to, once again, try to save their daughter. "I was bombarded with advice, much of it contradictory. I was advised to kick him out. I was advised not to let him out of my sight...His mother and I decided that we had to do everything possible to get Nick into a drug-rehabilitation program, so we researched them, calling recommended facilities, inquiring about their success rates for treating meth addicts. These conversations provided my initial glimpse of what must be the most chaotic, flailing field of health care in America."

The program Alyssa's parents settled on was a small, coed residential treatment center in Woodland Hills, California, known as Sober College. SoCo was cofounded by Cathy and Larry, a husband-and-wife team with ties to the Troubled Teen Industry. Larry had previously worked within the industry and carried with him several tenets from his time there. Primarily, how to handle SoCo's financials: making the program private and for-profit, with a $10,000-per-month price tag. But what was singular about the now-defunct SoCo was that it integrated college academics into the treatment, partnering with Woodbury University to create a pathway for patients to enroll at the school upon completion of the program. A choice that contributed to making SoCo the most overwhelmingly positive of the programs that I researched, one I believe was built on neither malice nor negligence.

Alyssa made friends easily at SoCo. Many of the other girls were also in recovery from hard drugs. Like Jenny, who had white-blond hair and had started using opioids with her older sister after their mother died of cancer. Or Natalie, whose shade of blond was more honey and who, like Alyssa, shot heroin. And Angie, the silky-black-haired daughter of an NBA player, who was the youngest of all of them and stuck to coke and Xanax. Between therapy and their classes, the four of them would hang out in the campus's designated smoking section. The large, purple booths that the students had desecrated with Sharpie graffiti. Tagging the weathering cushions with their initials, handles, and other lettering.

"Who's, like, your favorite musician of all time?" Alyssa asked the group.

"Ummm, I dunno. Why?" Jenny responded.

"I'm just so in love with Kurt Cobain right now."

"That dude that killed himself?"

"But, like, he was such a legend. He never stopped using, even when everyone wanted him to."

"Yeah."

Inevitably their conversations would turn into a war-storying session. Alyssa, Jenny, Natalie, and Angie taking turns recounting tales from their druggy days. Reflecting on the more outrageous, comical times. Or the heavenly annihilation of being high that made them all quietly twitch in their seats with longing. Alyssa's war stories usually centered on Owen. The two spoke from time to time, but with Alyssa on the other side of the country, they were no longer technically together. Still, she'd cry about him often.

One of the first *New York Times* op-eds I encountered of Maia Szalavitz's was the 2021 "Opioids Feel Like Love. That's Why They're Deadly in Tough Times."[1] Its examination of the brain opioid theory of social attachment makes me realize that for Alyssa, drugs and Owen were inextricably linked. As the 2021 article details, when nurturing a child or falling in love, oxytocin is released in the body, infusing memories of these experiences with calm and satisfaction. The same feelings opioids are able to elicit, as they mimic these very neurotransmitters. Imbuing Alyssa with the warmth, love, and safety she once felt with Owen, just from taking a hit.

"Fuck that dude," Natalie would remind her.

"He sounds like a total dick," Angie would agree.

"Hard agree," Jenny said.

Alyssa still couldn't stop the good memories from encroaching upon her. Like the time after she missed Elissa's funeral, Owen took her scrapbook and made a massive collage out of the photos for her wall. Or how he was there for her when she found out Elissa had died, comforting her as she cried.

"I know, I know. You're right," Alyssa said, willing herself to believe it.

At SoCo, Alyssa's days were filled with Narcotics Anonymous meetings, individual therapy sessions, college courses, and her volunteer work with animals. But Cathy and Larry also placed

an emphasis on learning how to have fun while sober. Allowing students to attend the large gatherings that their NA chapter would throw, like the white party that required them to all
dress in the color. In the photos I've seen from that night, Alyssa
wears a white, strapless dress paired with brown ankle-length
boots. Looking every bit the hot girl. And when Alyssa arrived
at the party, she took in the dance floor and bar of energy drinks
before discovering the hookah section, where she'd spend her
evening. She was never one for dancing, and certainly not while
sober.

While SoCo was coed, the staff policed the interactions between
the boys and the girls, discouraging romantic relationships. But
at the parties, they were free to flirt as they pleased. Though the
heroin had ravaged her body, leaving her even skinnier than she'd
been before it, her breasts were as large as ever. They wielded
the same power they had since sophomore year, beckoning all
the boys at the party to her. She was actively trying to move on
from Owen and allowed herself to flirt with the many boys she
met through SoCo and NA. They hung around her as they all
chugged six-packs of Red Bull, ate Clif Bars, and chain-smoked
cigarettes—their early recovery starter pack.

For a stretch of time Alyssa appeared to be making progress.
She got a job working retail and successfully convinced her parents to buy her a car to get to the store. She found herself a new
boyfriend, Dylan, who was also sober. Like Kenneth Rosen finding comfort in lockdown, institutionalization was what Alyssa
knew. It was where she thrived. Putting her head down, going
through the motions, inching her way toward more privileges. But

for those close to her, it was obvious. Sobriety wasn't what Alyssa wanted; what she wanted was another hit of that warmth, safety, and love.

———

The summer after my sophomore year, I discovered that my home friends had graduated from coke to opioids. I'd spent the first half of the summer interning in New York City, working at *Woman's Day*, the first stop on my quest to become an entertainment editor. When the internship was over, I went back to Providence for the month of August, hanging out with Gretchen and my Wheeler friends, Chloe and the rest of the sicko squad, and the group of private school boys we'd all started partying with more.

I'd always known some kids in Providence did Oxy. The story was typically the same: Some jock would tear their ACL and then start sharing their Oxy prescription with their friends as a treat, until the drugs became a mainstay among the group. Eventually leading them to heroin, getting the same high for a fraction of Oxy's price. While I'm not sure what exactly the impetus was behind my guy friends trying Oxy for the first time, their infiltration into our group followed a similar path. First Oxy was a thing Nick, Josh, and the others did in private—not bringing the pills to parties or talking openly about their use—but as August progressed, it had become a much more open secret.

One night, Gretchen and I went to a run-down nautical-themed dive bar with the sicko squad and the boys. We spent hours drinking watered-down well drinks on the back patio, beside the koi pond, where a rat had made itself a home among the fish. Whenever I spent time with Chloe, Sadie, and Violet, memories of Elissa made up the bulk of our conversation. At that point, I was still losing hours of my life to stalking her Facebook page, completely entrenched in her digital presence. It was a relief to talk about her in real life, and after a couple of hours of drinking and reminiscing, last call came—with half the group heading back to my house and the other heading to an undisclosed location, a place I didn't seem invited to.

"Come with us!" Violet called out to me as she, Chloe, and Sadie started walking off with Nick and Josh.

"Where to?" I asked.

"I'm sorry, but no," Josh said, pulling me aside. We'd known each other since middle school and there was an unspoken closeness between us, which he momentarily leaned on.

"I never, ever wanna see you doing this shit. It's not for you."

"No, I know. Thank you."

"Seriously, Sami."

Josh walked away, heading back to the group that was off to do Oxy, and as I headed home his words rang in my head. While Josh was an incredibly warm, well-natured guy, I'm still not quite sure why he pulled me aside that night. Why he felt so strongly that I shouldn't try the drugs that were slowly becoming so common among our friends. Why, once again, I was pulled away from the more dangerous, rebellious path. But regardless of his intentions, his message stuck with me. Never once feeling any temptation to try opioids or to be around them when they were used. A stance

I felt immense luck for having adopted in the years that followed. In the years when Oxy stopped being just a fun treat for many in my orbit. Leading them to heroin, addiction, rehab.

———

On the bus to Tarzana, Alyssa was sick with anticipation. The ride there from Woodland Hills was a quick fifteen minutes—both spots were in the Valley, just a stretch of sun-bleached storefronts and erstwhile shooting locations apart—but all Alyssa could focus on was her stomach-curdling impatience. What people often don't realize is that it's not the feeling of euphoria that draws many to heroin; it's the emotional relief it provides. Which is why research shows that those who have experienced childhood trauma—like Alyssa had, it being baked into the experience of therapeutic boarding school—are even more susceptible to opioid addiction. Alyssa was using to eradicate the anxiety and depression nothing else would stave off.

At SoCo, the administration handled their students' financials. Be it their paychecks or familial allowances, all money was fielded by the staff in order to eliminate any temptation to spend it on drugs. But somehow, by some godforsaken miracle, when Natalie's security deposit from her old apartment in Santa Barbara cleared, it was returned to her directly. Filling her bank account with more numbers than she or Alyssa—whom she'd confided in about the slipup—could comprehend. Each digit an individual sign from the universe urging them not to waste this opportunity.

Junkie logic encroaching upon their brains, telling them to go out and score.

Being relatively new to California, Alyssa wasn't tapped into its drug community quite yet. She'd visited Skid Row on SoCo's volunteer trips—passing out food to its unhoused population—but the idea of going there was gnarlier than she could wrap her head around. So they settled on calling Jenny, who had recently completed her stay at SoCo and was at sober living in Tarzana.

"Who is this?" Jenny said, having received a call from an unknown number.

"Alyssa!"

"Oh shit!"

"What are you doing today?"

"Not really sure. You?"

"Great. What do you think about Natalie and me rolling through?"

At first, Jenny was apprehensive. Though she was secretly abusing Mucinex—a popular crutch among not-quite-sober addicts, taking it for its dextromethorphan, which didn't show up on drug tests—she truly had a year clean off heroin. She'd also only ever tried white powder heroin, not the black tar variety that came from Mexico and was much more popular on the West Coast. Its dark orange, sticky substance scared her. Unsure of how it would make her feel, or how much her body could handle. But Alyssa and Natalie's junkie logic had enraptured Jenny as well, and before she knew it, she was agreeing to meet them at the nearby bus stop.

"What's the plan?!" Alyssa asked once they'd reunited.

"There's this pharmacy dude," Jenny said.

"Works for me," Natalie said.

"We gotta catch the metro to get to him, though," Jenny said.

"Cool," Alyssa said.

While at Pitzer, I'd make the occasional trip into Los Angeles to either visit my cool California cousins or attend a concert. One of my first times in, I took the metro from downtown Los Angeles to Santa Monica and quickly learned why the city's public transportation system is so neglected. The stops were erratic, the maps indecipherable to my untrained eye. And taking the orange line to meet the pharmaceutical dude, Alyssa and the other girls were plagued by the same incomprehension, ultimately getting off at the wrong stop and having to walk the remainder of the way.

"Actually, I don't know about this," Jenny said, not long into the trek.

"Like he's not holding?" Alyssa asked.

"No, no. You're all good. I just dunno if I'm all good."

"Ooooooh."

"I'm not gonna rat on you guys or anything. Like, totally do your thing."

"All right, then. Thank you."

"Yeah, of course."

Heading back to sober living, Jenny stayed true to her word. Alyssa and Natalie had signed out of SoCo on the two-hour passes the students were permitted. But once those two hours came and went, the staff began calling Jenny, suspicious that she might have a sense of what had gone down, grilling her about their whereabouts. Yet all Jenny told them was that she'd heard they were somewhere in the Valley, nothing more, nothing less. Things were different from all the other times Alyssa had tried to escape. While her parents had urged her to attend SoCo, Alyssa was now a legal adult and had consented to the program. Though Cathy and Larry could worry about Alyssa and call around looking for her, it was just as much her right to run off and relapse as it was to enroll in SoCo in the first place.

Somewhere deep in the Valley, Alyssa and Natalie were holed up in a hotel room, running through their newly procured supply. Alyssa had been clean for a while, with her physiological tolerance having deteriorated since her days of shooting up in Owen's attic. But she and Natalie prepared themselves for their decline in stamina, having purchased Narcan and treating it like steroids—something to revive them and allow them to continue using, far past the limitations their own bodies had imposed upon them.

Each part of the shooting-up process electrified Alyssa. Dissolving the drug down into liquid ember. The seconds before her brain caught up to the chemical infusion. The moment her body finally gave over to it, becoming sweaty and slouchy. She and Natalie taking turns, edging right up until the point of overdose, then administering the Narcan. Bringing each other back to life just to make vampires of themselves once more.

––––––––––

Alyssa's relapse had relatively few consequences. She hadn't been arrested while out buying drugs, or during the many hours she spent in the hotel room, fading in and out of consciousness. When she was done, she simply elected to go back to SoCo, resuming treatment.

While this was partially luck, it also has everything to do with the nature of the opioid crisis itself. According to a study published in *JAMA Psychiatry*, nearly 90 percent of the people who tried heroin for the first time between 2004 and 2014 were white, with the average heroin user being a twenty-three-year-old white woman.[2] Statistics that stand in stark contrast to the racial makeup of the typical heroin user fifty years prior, which was a sixteen-year-old Black male. Leading the face of opioid addiction to become white, middle- to upper-class suburbanites. A face like Alyssa's.

The opioid epidemic is far from the first drug crisis to ravage America. In the 1980s and early '90s, crack cocaine claimed thousands of American lives per year, many of which came from the Black community. In response, the government criminalized addiction, taking what became called a "tough on crime" approach, passing laws to lock up those who used and sold drugs, and employing mandatory minimum sentences. The 1990s also birthed the meth epidemic—which primarily affected working-class white Americans in the Southwest—and was met with the same "tough on crime" treatment.

Yet lawmakers and government officials have approached the opioid crisis in a much more compassionate way, considering it to be a public health issue and treating it as such. Congress has allocated $1 billion to combating the crisis and emphasizing the necessity of prioritizing treatment over incarceration. This decision is rooted in racial bias, because as the Vox article "When a

Drug Epidemic's Victims Are White" reported, the majority of lawmakers are also affluent and white, which causes them to have further compassion for a population of addicts made up of people who look like them, and a disease that is likely to impact their friends, families, and communities. It has also resulted in laws and regulations that Alyssa ultimately benefited from, not being flanked by police officers out trolling the streets, targeting young white women, looking to imprison them. All of this allowed her to reenter rehab without any greater punishment—no matter how many times she relapsed.

CHAPTER XVIII

Alissa

Alissa and Anthony moved fast. Within a year they'd started living together, got engaged, and conceived a child. It was a big change for a twenty-year-old and her first boyfriend. But Alissa welcomed the warp speed at which adulthood was coming her way. After Ponca Pines, she'd been faced with the same binary that Elissa had grappled with. That choice to either move forward as a reformed woman or return to life as a troubled teen. While Elissa and Alyssa had gravitated toward the latter—with Alissa still regularly talking to Alyssa from rehab, hearing firsthand about the fallout from Alyssa's regression—she tried to remake herself in the Troubled Teen Industry's ideal image: going to AA meetings, procuring a job as a hostess, and preparing for the arrival of her child. Doing everything she could to be a good girl, no longer a good-time girl.

It helped that Alissa loved being pregnant. The hormones that newly flooded her body softened her, temporarily tempering that tempestuous streak. She'd become more affectionate, constantly wanting to cuddle with Anthony. Pawing at him around others with little regard for people's lack of patience for PDA. The promise of new life had filled Alissa with hope. After months of mourning Elissa all over the internet, Alissa's grief was beginning to relent. Even the tenor of her posts on Elissa's wall began to change. They were filled with contentment, like the one that read: *There's nothing I would change right now in my life ... except to have my twin back in this world.*

Henry was born in December 2012, coming out with Alissa's aquamarine eyes and her unruly hair. She quickly took to being a mother, taking elaborate Facebook photo shoots of Henry dressed in gingham button-up shirts and miniature jeans that made him look like a mid-level manager in his business casual attire. Or bringing him to play with her older sister Mary's three daughters, who doted on the newest addition to their family. Alissa was also still close to Halle, who had discovered that she was pregnant just one month after Alissa delivered. And with the arrival of Halle's son, the two of them became mom friends. Hanging out, ordering excessive amounts of food from Pizza Hut, and binge-watching *Shameless* while their kids slept soundly beside them. Their friendship now peaceful and PG.

Meanwhile, I was in my sophomore year of college and nowhere close to moving on from my grief. I hid it well from my friends at school, fearing I'd maxed out on my lifetime allotment of emotional support from them. I'd gone back into therapy, talking to my childhood psychologist over the phone, before quickly abandoning treatment. Not yet ready to do the work. Instead, I started talking to Campbell again, who was now living in New York and far enough away from me that I felt free to reveal myself. I remember once calling him crying as I paced up and down a train platform. He kept assuring me, *You'll be okay, you'll feel better soon, it just takes time.* Platitudes that made me snap and tell him that I didn't want to move on. That I didn't want to forget the way her nose wrinkled when she smiled or all her freckles no amount of concealer could hide. But what I didn't realize at the time was that holding on to my grief over Elissa was a way to still hold on to her. My sadness serving as my tether.

Though Alissa showed off her happy family all over Facebook, she was also still struggling. By the next year Anthony tells me that their relationship had begun to falter. They fought for months on end—both about the normal things new parents fight about, as well as those singular to them as a couple—until he ultimately moved out of Alissa's mother's basement, where they'd been raising Henry. Still, they weren't quite broken up. More so *not together, but not, not together.* Stuck in a liminal state, until Alissa invited Anthony to spend the day at Omaha's Zorinsky Lake with Henry, Mary, and her daughters.

While visitors are prohibited from swimming in the lake itself, what brings Nebraskans to Zorinsky is its 255 acres of recreational space. The fishing dock, playgrounds, baseball diamonds, hiking trails, and water park where Anthony, Alissa, Mary, and the kids set up shop for the day. Mary's three girls were the right age to fully take advantage of the park's pool and towering water slides, whereas Alissa and Anthony took turns tending to the now two-year-old Henry. These were the days when Anthony felt most hopeful. Watching Alissa care for Henry, he couldn't help but place more emphasis on the *not, not together* nature of their arrangement.

"I think I'm gonna take him in the pool," Alissa said.

"Need anything?" Anthony asked.

"No, I think we're good. Aren't we, Henry?"

"Cool, I'm just gonna hang in the shade."

"Sounds good."

Anthony sat back with the group's belongings. The damp towels, sweaty water bottles, and other detritus of a perfect summer day. And somewhere in the mess of water park gear, Alissa's phone started lighting up, displaying a series of text messages from a number Anthony didn't recognize. Watching them pour in reminded Anthony of another text he'd received earlier in the day, from his weed dealer. *Your baby mama came by to pick up.* A message that, just a few hours before, had annoyed him. *Alissa had been with him all morning, getting Henry ready for the water park. Not off buying drugs*, he thought. But between the two sets of texts, suspicions began worming their way around Anthony's brain. Realizing that maybe it hadn't been some big misunderstanding; maybe he had been the one to misunderstand.

Anthony wasn't naive to the fact that Alissa had started getting fucked up again. Once Alissa's maternity leave ended, she started a new job in guest services at the Marriott. To her surprise, she got a thrill out of mitigating the petty conflicts of the pissed-off guests. She also loved her coworkers, who were all young, fun, and down to party. But the temptation to join them taunted her. Her high school career, along with her college one, had been cut short. As had her adolescence, ending the day she decided to have

Henry. There was a part of her that felt like she'd been so good for so long that she was owed a chance to let loose. The troubled teen was still dormant inside her, ready for a reprise. And as she started hanging out with the Marriott gang more and more, her time with them started bleeding into her fights with Anthony. He was distrustful of Hazel, her closest friend at the hotel, and the others she hung out with late into the night. Suspicious of Alissa, and the extent of her partying, as well.

Back at the lake, Anthony tried to silence his worries. Attempting not to think about the Marriott or the texts. Alissa and Mary had started packing up for the day, getting the kids ready to head back to Mary's house for a big dinner. Alissa had invited one of her high school friends, Riley, to join them for the evening. Just like during her teen years in her basement, Alissa still loved having people around. Inviting them to come hang with her and Henry, injecting into family gatherings her friends from her many walks of life. But by this point, the majority of Alissa's friends weren't exactly Team Anthony. Having heard about one too many of their screaming matches. And as they were on the precipice of yet another one, Riley appeared visibly annoyed. Rolling her eyes and riling Anthony up even further.

"Alissa, can we talk for a second?" Anthony asked.

"What's up?" Alissa responded.

"Why does something need to be up?"

"Guess it doesn't."

Mary's house was in a state of chaos. In one room, she and her husband were sorting out dinner. In another, Alissa's mother was watching over all of her grandchildren, while Riley was hovering around Alissa and Anthony, poised to jump in and defend her friend. So Anthony ushered Alissa out to the back porch, in the hopes of finding some privacy.

"What's Riley doing rolling her eyes at me?" Anthony asked.

"She wasn't. Chill out," Alissa said.

"I don't think you're being straight with me."

"About what?"

"Like, who's blowing up your phone?"

"Nobody's blowing up my phone—"

"Bullshit."

It was a variation on the many fights they'd had before. While Anthony was trying to hold on to their relationship, Alissa was once again moving forward at warp speed. Though she loved being a mom, she was no longer interested in the fantasy family life she'd built. Suddenly eager to blow it all up, in order to revert back to being the troubled teen she'd tried so hard to evolve past. And just as their fight began to crescendo, Riley descended on the porch. Ready to play intermediary.

"Dude, you need to calm down," Riley said.

"Like this is any of your fucking business," Anthony said.

"You're gonna let him be rude to me?" Riley asked Alissa.

"Anthony, leave her alone," Alissa said.

"I'm sick of this shit. I'm leaving," Anthony said.

Anthony stormed off, leaving Alissa free to answer the barrage of texts he'd been so incensed by. Those that came from Reg, the new guy she'd been seeing.

If Anthony was the embodiment of the stable life she'd once wanted, Reg had become the paragon of all the excitement she was craving. And along with being the symbolic inverses of each other, the two were also physical opposites. Reg was a short, light-skinned Black man with a six-pack and lean limbs. He was a year younger than Alissa, and those close to Alissa say he also dealt drugs. (Reg himself hasn't responded to my attempts at outreach, living a relatively off-the-grid life.) Members of Alissa's friends and family consider him to be the kind of guy who did a bit of this, a bit of that, amassing just as much money as he needed to keep his partying going, but contribute to little else. Alissa met Reg through Hazel and was instantly infatuated. After having Henry, Alissa's anorexia resurfaced. She became obsessed with eliminating the extra rim of fat that still rounded her face, the pockets of flesh that had yet to flatten near her pelvis. And while Anthony had made her feel desired, to be wanted by someone she found as hot as Reg felt like the antidote to her poor self-esteem. They began sleeping together and eventually started dating. She'd just yet to tell Anthony.

The morning after the fight, Anthony showed up at Claire's house to grab some of the clothes he'd left behind. Still mad about all that had transpired, Anthony headed down the stairs to the basement, looking to make a show of collecting his belongings. While Alissa was pregnant, Anthony and his father had given the basement a partial remodel. Walking through it now, Anthony took in the work they'd done. The hardwood mahogany floors they'd installed. The various Disney character decals they'd plastered all over the walls and glow-in-the-dark stars they'd hung on the ceiling—all to ready themselves for Henry. Then he kept on walking toward Alissa's bedroom, where he could hear her stirring.

"What the fuck?" Anthony said after opening the door.

"Fuck. Hi," Alissa said.

" 'Sup, man," Reg said, rolling over.

Reg took up the majority of the bed, with Alissa sitting up by the pillows, her body draped in the sheets. Anthony stared at them blankly, taking in the face on the other side of the texts. Alissa appeared disheveled, the black eyeliner she was so heavy-handed with having made its way down her cheeks. Anthony had seen her high before—they'd occasionally smoked weed and drank together, though not to excess—but the way those aquamarine eyes seemed awash in fog was something he'd never seen before. And beneath her, by the foot of the bed, Henry occupied himself with a toy left on the floor. Too absorbed in his own world to take note of the adults.

"Fuck this. I'm done," Anthony said.

"Okay," Alissa said.

"I mean it this time."

"Fine by me."

True to his word, Anthony stopped pursuing Alissa, only communicating with her for coparenting purposes, continuing to maintain his presence in Henry's life. Alissa was now free to be with Reg and embrace all his lifestyle had to offer. She'd been doing opioids behind Anthony's back for a while now. Her pregnancy had exacerbated an old cheerleader injury, messing with the curvature of her spine. And when she went to the doctor to have it checked out, she left with a prescription for painkillers. Drugs that filled her with the same feeling all that binge-drinking had years prior: a comfortableness in her own skin. She also had started using with her friends at the Marriott, on those nights out with Hazel that Anthony had been so wary of. But now dating Reg, her world became subsumed by the Oxy and hydrocodone she used. And later on, fentanyl.

Sometime after Ponca Pines, Alissa was diagnosed with bipolar disorder. A condition that seemed to make sense of her proclivity for violence, as well as the fury with which she took to opioids. In 2021, the National Institutes of Health issued a study on the link between bipolar disorder and comorbid use of illicit substances.[1] And while they weren't able to determine why people with BD are at higher risk for addictive disorders, they found common neurobiological and genetic underpinnings and epigenetic alterations between the two, determining that as a consequence, 56 percent of subjects with BD also suffer from substance abuse disorders, Alissa being one of them.

But also, like with Alyssa, opioids had become integral to her relationship with Reg. For all the inherent danger of such a dynamic, it's one that Hollywood has anointed as sexy. Movies that imprinted on me like Heath Ledger's *Candy*, the love story between a junkie poet and a junkie art student. Or *Drugstore Cowboy*, in which Matt Dillon and Kelly Lynch play a couple of addicts who rob pharmacies up and down the Pacific Northwest to support their habit. While the films are meant to be cautionary tales, the eroticism of the relationships they depict is undeniable. How rooted in desire they are: for drugs, sex, a life of total carnality. I even enacted this dynamic, on a much smaller scale, in my own fledgling love life. After having lured in Campbell with lorazepam, I repeated the tactic in college, using coke as a way to flirt with my crush, whom I'd exchange knowing glances with before slinking off together to do blow. Our own version of foreplay.

For a while, Alissa and Reg sustained this dynamic, moving into Claire's basement. Alissa was so relieved to no longer have to keep their relationship confined to the shadows. Thrilled to fully claim this man whom she was so attracted to, whom she was so enthralled by. She started showing him off on Facebook. Pictures that I pore through now, from a professional photo shoot they did together, for which Reg wore a black baseball cap and a mono-chrome flannel. In them, he has his arm draped over Alissa, who appears more angular than in any prior photos I've seen of her. Gone are any traces of jowls, any chub on her arms. Just the two of them, smiling directly into the camera.

Then two landmark life events coincided for the couple: Alissa got pregnant and Reg turned twenty-one. Her pregnancy with Henry had filled her with so much positivity that she allowed memories of that time to buoy her as she decided to keep the child. While Alissa started putting in the work to get sober, Reg was even more eager to party than ever. Now that he was of legal drinking age, all he wanted to do was hit the bars. He started staying out late, without Alissa. A new dynamic began to pre-sent itself in their relationship, one in which she'd become the Anthony, embodying all his jealousies she'd so resented. Suddenly suspicious of where Reg had been, whom he'd been with.

"All right. I'm gonna head out," Reg said one afternoon, hang-ing out on the couch in the basement.

"What the fuck? Where are you going?" Alissa asked.

"Just meeting up with some people."

"Are you serious right now?"

"...Yes?"

"Fuck you."

"Fuck me?"

"Yes."

"Wow. Fuck this, I'm out of here."

Alissa's pregnancy aside, there were different societal expectations placed on her and Reg when it came to sobriety. In Kimberly Sue's 2019 *Getting Wrecked: Women, Incarceration, and the American Opioid Crisis*, she points out the double standard of addiction, claiming that women's drug use, particularly white women's, disturbs society much more than men's. Because women are or have the potential to become mothers, we moralize their drug use. Stoking our culture's obsession with women as keepers of the domestic realm and our subsequent desire to penalize any woman who deviates from this role.

Sue explains that this societal response is in keeping with the judgment women face anytime they stray from the hallmarks of upper-middle-class white morality. Chastising them for using drugs in the same way we do for getting divorced, having an abortion, or exhibiting lewd behavior. But as Alissa saw firsthand, this moralizing isn't just reserved for adults. It's also inflicted on teenage girls who behave "badly." Alissa had faced this wrath ever since her adolescence. Having been subjected to an entire industry fueled by this philosophy: that those who are rebellious are bad and must be fixed. A lifetime of being judged, ostracized, and punished for the impulses deep within her that she couldn't silence.

CHAPTER XIX

Alyssa

While Alyssa craved freedom, each time she had a taste of it, she was met with the same outcome. Getting sober only to start using again, then using enough to end up back at SoCo or sober living. Alyssa's stints on the outside never lasted long. Her friends estimate that her longest stretch of sobriety lasted seventy days. The recursive nature of Alyssa's life took a toll on her. Friends say she looked like she'd lost upward of twenty pounds, with track marks tracing the crooks of her arms, the skin surrounding the puncture wounds having turned a faint shade of gray.

When speaking with Alyssa's friends about this time in her life, my thoughts keep returning to Larry Clark's 1971 photobook, *Tulsa*. The controversial collection offers sixty-four pages of black-and-white photographs of young midwestern adults in various states of shooting up and being strung out. Though it isn't the grainy, gritty images themselves—whether it is a guy injecting his topless girlfriend with heroin or a pregnant mother with a syringe in her arm—that leave me so unsettled. It's the last line of Clark's introduction: *Once the needle goes in, it never comes out.*

The summer before my senior year in Providence, of all my home friends who got into Oxy, two caught the bug the worst. Nick, the party boy whom Violet had been seeing; and Kieran, whom Gretchen would sleep with when we came home for the summers. They were the ringleaders of our revelry. I'd host them in my basement, where they'd perform the macarena for us at four o'clock in the morning or swing dance with me to the Beach Boys' "Don't Worry Baby."

By that summer, they'd replaced Oxy with heroin, shedding the rambunctious, merrymaking energy that had so endeared them to me as they sequestered themselves away. Using instead of partying. Watching them become shadows of their former selves was trying on all of us. Igniting that helper's instinct within me, itchy and sick with my desire to be the one to solely rise to the occasion and save them. Instead, it was a group effort. Interventions were staged, serious talks were had, and ultimately, Nick got help, having maintained his sobriety ever since, while Kieran's battle with addiction still rages on, his fight against the same demons Alyssa was up against.

To Kieran, being an addict was romantic. After his parents offered him an ultimatum—get clean or get out—he opted for homelessness, loitering around near his parents' summer home, sleeping under a dumpster. Going to rehab only to start sharing needles with his friends in his halfway house. To us, he seemed to get off on the pain and suffering as much as the high itself. Same as Alyssa did, in her god worship of Kurt Cobain and his commitment to drugs. Molding herself in his image. Telling friends she didn't think she'd make it to thirty, and that she wasn't even entirely sure she'd want to.

Though Kieran's addiction journey gave me a better understanding of Alyssa's, what I still didn't comprehend were the physiological forces keeping them in the throes of addiction. In *Getting Wrecked*, Sue also writes about a new line of thought in addiction studies. Focusing on the rise of researchers who now view addiction as a chronic disease that damages users by destroying their dopamine receptors. Some even going so far as to propose that we view addiction as a developmental disorder, such as ADHD, autism spectrum disorder, or any others that are the result of genetic and personality components paired with environmental developmental conditions. Wreaking havoc on those like Alyssa and Kieran, who had gotten so accustomed to the complete decimation of heroin that no other feeling of pleasure existed to them.

———

Alyssa first met Jasper at SoCo. By the time he got there, he had six years of addiction under his belt. His breaking point came when he lost his passport in Southeast Asia and proceeded to stay for six months, riding out a heroin bender. Alyssa was doing well when she and Jasper reconnected. They were both out of SoCo and staying at different sober living facilities. Alyssa was dog sitting to make money and wanted to become a veterinary assistant. The two started dating, enmeshing themselves in the young persons' AA scene in Los Angeles. Going to meetings, then loitering at nearby cafés with the rest of their group. Chain-smoking and ordering as little as they could without getting kicked out. Dating in sober living had its challenges. Alyssa and Jasper both had roommates and weren't allowed to go into each other's bedrooms. The only places they could hook up were in Alyssa's Kia or in unpopulated outdoor spaces. Vacant baseball fields and the like.

Jasper was serious about his sobriety. As much as he liked Alyssa, sometimes when he looked at her all he could see was how uncomfortable she was in her skin when sober. How her yearning for heroin radiated off her, so potent that Jasper worried it might infect him. Scared that if they stayed together, they'd pull each other right back down. About three or four months into the relationship, Jasper ended things.

The two remained friends, even after Alyssa relapsed. Jasper was living in an apartment by then, and occasionally Alyssa would call him at odd hours. Never asking him for help outright, just allowing a sense of urgency to linger in the air. One that Jasper was fluent in and responded to in kind. He'd pick her up from random hotels, like the one she'd been holed up in near Northridge, to come crash at his place.

"Hey," Alyssa said.

"Been awhile. You good?" Jasper asked.

"I guess..."

"Where are you?"

"Northridge or something. I'll text you?"

"Please do."

Alyssa was alone when Jasper got there. Having snuck away from the group she'd come with, beelining to his car. Once she got inside, all Jasper could focus on was her eyes. Wide and wily, flitting around as she examined the dashboard, steering wheel, and upholstery. Alyssa couldn't seem to steady her gaze or slow the jittering of her limbs. Sometime on the drive she admitted to having mixed heroin and meth. In the wake of her confession, Jasper realized how frightened she appeared. How scared she was to be so out of control as she convulsed and cried throughout their drive home.

Back at Jasper's, they stayed up through the night talking. When Jasper first met Alyssa, she came off as that shy, guarded girl she'd presented as since childhood. At SoCo, she'd never voluntarily share in group meetings, developing a reputation for being closed-off and noncompliant with the program. Once they started dating, she came out of her shell more. Revealing herself to be a loud, opinionated young woman with a seriously funny streak. But in all her opening up, Jasper had never seen her be quite as vulnerable as she was that night. Crying as she talked in circles, repeating again and again how frustrated she was by all her self-sabotage. Sharing that she couldn't imagine herself as an *adult*. Too paralyzed by the transition from adolescence to adulthood, too lacking in the tools necessary to make the leap to even fathom outgrowing her youth.

"I was such a wreck before. You have no idea," Jasper said.

"As bad as me?" Alyssa asked.

"Worse. It took me so many tries to get here."

"I've started over so many times now."

"I know, but you gotta want it. You gotta want to get better."

"I do, I do."

"Then you'll do it. Trust me."

Jasper spent the night walking Alyssa through his journey to recovery. Sharing all his false starts, relapses, and do-overs. Talking at her instead of to her, because Alyssa was crying too hard to take anything in. Shaking and sobbing until the sun came up and she agreed to go back to sober living. As Jasper drove her to the facility, it was impossible to discern who believed Alyssa would get it together less. Jasper, pumping Alyssa up, trying to will her into recovery; or Alyssa, playing along, half-heartedly soaking up his words of encouragement.

"You've got this," Jasper said.

"You think?" Alyssa asked.

"I believe in you."

"That means a lot to me. For real."

"Of course."

Embarking on yet another attempt to get sober, Alyssa seemed to have little faith in herself. There were a number of factors working against her. Both her resignation to the life as well as the physiological challenges stacked against her as a woman suffering from substance abuse disorder.

The Substance Abuse Mental-Health Services Administration found that women become dependent on drugs more quickly, particularly in the case of opioids. And according to a study from the NIH called "Sex Differences, Gender and Addiction," women have a harder time quitting heroin and are more susceptible to relapse than men.[1] This is likely because women experience greater withdrawal responses and are more sensitive to stress and other common relapse triggers. Findings that Alyssa embodied, not lasting long at the facility that Jasper dropped her off at, instead going back to the streets to seek that all-powerful high. Alyssa was fairly off the grid in the following months, with Jasper losing tabs on her, until he got the call in which he found out that Alyssa's premonition had come true. She'd overdosed, not making it past twenty-three.

Alyssa's friends have different recollections of the circumstances surrounding her death. While they'd all been close friends at SoCo, their sobriety journeys had taken them in different directions, with Alyssa isolating herself from many as she descended further and further into addiction. So when they found out about Alyssa's passing, the information they received was mere gossip.

Jasper was of the belief that she was at a hotel not unlike the one he picked her up at that night in Northridge. All alone in the room when the needle went in for the final time. Another friend from SoCo recalled a much more dramatic set of events. According to her, Alyssa had been using with a group of people who drove her to the hospital after she overdosed. When they arrived, they dropped her body off at the front entrance, speeding off without any regard for whether or not she was successfully resuscitated. When I speak with Jasper about Alyssa's death, he sends me over the lyrics to a song he wrote at the time. "The Door in the Floor," a track that embodies the contradictions he feels. Both glad that she's at peace and devastated to lose yet another person to this disease. *Baby I can't feel the pain of breaking down my soul anymore. The rushing of the train in my veins is creaking to a*

*stop O my lord. It's all right leaves in flight, just tell my parents when
their hearts are sore. The TV's all right you'll be fine. She doesn't cry
anymore.*

Nearly a year into my looking into Alyssa's life and death, I was
able to track down her autopsy report. The outline of Alyssa's life
her mother had shared with me stopped soon after Alyssa became
addicted to heroin, ending with the note: "We would discover
that the Addiction Treatment Industry in this country has much
in common with the Troubled Teen Industry, but that is another
story and I don't have the energy to tell it right now."

But the twenty-seven-page autopsy report lays bare the details
of her death that Louise wasn't able to share with me: *23-year-old
female reportedly found unresponsive in a bathtub at a residence (not
submerged)*, the first page reads in tidy, methodical handwriting.
In the following pages, the medical examiner writes that there
weren't any signs of trauma or foul play. Other than gray ecchymo-
sis by the punctate erythematous and the markings of an appen-
dectomy, her body was free of abnormalities. Or as the autopsy
put it, her organs and various body parts were "unremarkable."

During much of my investigation, I prided myself on my ability to desensitize myself to the often difficult, disconcerting truths
I was learning. Usually able to listen to the abuses that Elissa and
her friends suffered at the hands of the Troubled Teen Industry, as
well as the abuses they inflicted on themselves in the wake of their
time within it, without flinching. Still valuing my ability to handle
the hard stuff, rather than pushing myself to work through what
I took on. But when reading Alyssa's autopsy report, I couldn't
seem to shake it off. Including the page that detailed the weight

of her spleen, described her endometrium as "not thickened," and categorized her abdomen as flat.

At first my interest in Alissa and Alyssa was primarily in service to learning more about Elissa. Wanting to know the effects their friendships had on my friend, rather than on one another. But as I've gone deeper and deeper down the rabbit hole, tracing Alyssa's life far past the time she spent with Elissa, the more I carry her with me as well. Tormented by the same conflicting and confounding feelings that plague Jasper and so many of the others who cared for her. Relieved that Alyssa finally found peace, while also devastated she was unable to do so on this earth.

———————

There were two memorials held for Alyssa: one at SoCo and another in Northbrook. Cathy often held the funerals of former patients at her facility. Never shying away from the dark realities of addiction. Eager to send the message *If you don't get your shit together, addiction will kill you.* Along with the other, more pointed lesson that she shares with me: *Rich junkies might have more resources, but they end up dead too.*

The interior walls of the main building on SoCo's campus were plastered in portraits of former students. Those who attended the program and had died of the disease. And at Alyssa's funeral, she had various photos of her time at SoCo blown up and displayed on easels, one of which would later go on the wall, alongside all the others.

Today, overdoses kill more Americans annually than gun violence, car accidents, or breast cancer. As a result, Cathy had funerals down to a science, knowing exactly what snacks to get, which flowers to buy. How to get the word out to those who were still in the LA area, like Jasper, to come and pay their respects. The reception itself was exceedingly adequate. Alyssa's body had been sent back to Northbrook, so the mourners communed around the photographs as stand-ins. For those who weren't particularly close to Alyssa, the conversation primarily consisted of small talk. She'd been so guarded at SoCo that many of her classmates felt like they hadn't gotten to know her. Even the photographs that Cathy was able to track down were mostly of Alyssa in the background. Shirking group activities, unwilling to smile for the camera.

"Fuck, man," one mourner said.

"Totally awful," said another.

"Her poor family."

"Seriously."

The mourners were all just going through the motions, having become too desensitized to death to truly grieve Alyssa. Alyssa's was just another in the long line of services they'd been to. Knowing all too well that they'd all be at SoCo again, laying to rest another friend.

That refrain I heard time and time again in action: *You don't go to weddings or birthdays. Just funerals.*

Back in Northbrook, her mother, Louise, relied on the tenets of the Jewish faith for how to arrange Alyssa's funeral. Planning a graveside service and a shiva to follow. Thinking of Louise in those moments, I return again to a passage from Sheff's "My Addicted Son": "Through Nick's drug addiction, I learned that parents can bear almost anything. Every time we reach a point where we feel as if we can't bear any more, we do. Things had descended in a way that I never could have imagined, and I shocked myself with my ability to rationalize and tolerate things that were once unthinkable."

At the funeral itself, many hovered around Louise. People like Kate, who, despite having drifted apart from Alyssa in high school—when Alyssa started partying and Kate neglected to—had kept up her ties to Louise. Inquiring about how Alyssa was doing and checking in on their family. At the burial, Kate stood behind Louise, rubbing her shoulders. Sitting with her at the shiva, looking through the scrapbook Louise had made of her favorite photos of Alyssa.

"Look how happy she looks here," Louise said.

"She looks beautiful," Kate said.

"She really was. Wasn't she?"

"Absolutely."

"It helps. Remembering the good times."

"Of course."

Talking to Kate about the funeral, her words echo the same sentiment that is so immured in my grief over Elissa: guilt. The last time Kate had spoken to Alyssa was about a year prior to her death. She had reached out to her on Facebook to tell her that she was coming to California. They discussed hanging out, but when the time came, Kate was afraid to push it. Full of the same insecurities that I'd had: worried Alyssa might not actually want to see her, that she'd be overdoing it if she tried that hard to meet up. She didn't think too much about it, until a year later. When a Facebook post that read *RIP Alyssa* popped up on her timeline.

Kate wonders aloud whether or not Alyssa knew how much she cared about her. To which my impulse is to console her. Reminding her that Alyssa absolutely knew she loved her, that she has nothing to feel guilty about, and that she couldn't have saved her. And as I tell her this, I start to cry. Loud, unrelenting tears that I try to muffle while apologizing profusely into the phone. Different from any of the tears I've cried over Elissa before, ones that are unfamiliar to me. It's as if in hearing the advice I'm giving to Kate, I'm speaking to a part of me that needs to absorb it as well. My body finally starting to expel even a piece of the grief and the guilt that I've held so tight to—now over all three girls. Tears not of devastation, but of release.

CHAPTER XX

Alissa

A lissa's daughter, Faith, was born with light brown skin, curly black hair, and her mother's facial expressions. Alissa's wide mouth and eyes that scrunched up into crescent moons when smiling. Faith's birth filled Alissa with a new sense of commitment to getting sober. Admitting herself to Immanuel Medical Center's mental health unit, where she could get straight. Alissa felt comfortable at Immanuel; there was a program director named Joan she was fond of, and for a period of time Alissa was in and out of their care. Staying at Immanuel for three or so weeks, checking out, relapsing, then going back to the unit.

Save for a sixty-day stay at a rehab facility in Maryland, Alissa's life was confined to this cycle. When not in treatment she primarily lived with Reg, whose drug use continued to be a problem in their relationship. As was their incessant fighting. The two would fight, break up, and then Alissa would use to cope. Or they'd get back together, and Alissa would begin using again with him. It was a cycle not unlike the one Alyssa had found herself in. Until Alyssa's passing, Alissa called her regularly, both confiding in each other about their struggles with sobriety. Alissa would then write on Elissa's wall, sharing updates from their calls like, *"We're both almost 2 months sober by the grace of god and by you!!! Thank u so much Elissa u are by far the best guardian angel anybody could ask for."*

That Reg was emotionally abusive was no secret to Alissa's friends. Amy had witnessed enough of the fights Reg and Alissa would get into. The way he'd hit below the belt, needling away at Alissa's greatest insecurities. Heightening her anxieties about what he would do when he went out, the other women he'd meet. Sometimes Alissa would suggest to Amy that the abuse would cross the line from emotional into physical. Amy didn't know what to believe. Alissa's emotions had grown so extreme since she'd started using, with her memories so clouded by the high. Amy understood what little grasp addicts often had on reality and wasn't sure if the allegations were just Alissa's addiction talking— until Henry, who was now seven, was able to confirm them.

One night, Alissa had accused Reg of dipping into her bank account to buy drugs. The stealing pissed her off, but his refusal to share the supply enraged her even further. A fight broke out, the details of which have become hazy to those closest to Alissa in the ensuing years. The particular acts of violence that occurred now having been lost to the passage of time, mixed in with all the other fights, and all the other trouble Reg had wreaked. Instead, they only remember the fallout of this incident. As Claire tells it, Child Protective Services came to Alissa and Reg's apartment, and when they questioned Henry, he was able to corroborate the information CPS had received. Both Faith and Henry were taken from Alissa and placed in Mary's care. In turn, Alissa finally, truly had hit rock bottom.

———————

Claire wasn't surprised that Alissa was running late. She was chronically scatterbrained. Always losing her cell phone or keys, never paying punctuality much mind. On this particular morning, she was even more frazzled than Claire was accustomed to. Sitting in the front seat of her mother's car, she radiated anxiety. Looking at herself in the mirror, smoothing the flyaways out of her hair, and then turning around to the back seat to tinker with Faith's outfit.

"Can we swing by Walmart on the way?" Alissa asked.

"We're gonna be cutting it close," Claire said.

"No, no. We have to. I need pants."

"What about what you're wearing?"

"It's all wrong!"

They were coming from Better Together, the sober living facility Alissa had been staying at in the months after the CPS call. The program had come highly recommended, as it was known for helping parents recover and regain custody of their children. As Claire remembers it, it was staffed by a fleet of social workers, therapists, and peer support specialists who guided patients through the arduous and often heavily bureaucratic reunification process.

Alissa had committed herself fully to the program. Moving into an apartment on the premises without Reg, regularly submitting herself to urine tests, going for methadone treatment. Claire visited the facility regularly. Attending family group therapy sessions with Alissa, sitting in on her meetings with the staff, educating herself on what the state would require of her daughter. Drug counselors will often repeat "the Three C's" to parents: "You didn't cause it, you can't control it, and you can't cure it." But Claire couldn't help herself from trying to cure Alissa. At Better Together, Claire was moved by what an active participant Alissa was being in the whole process. How seriously Alissa was taking Better Together, the way she seemed willing to do whatever it would take to get Henry and Faith back.

After five months of treatment—and five months of sobriety—Alissa finally had her chance. Leaving Walmart, Claire and Alissa made their way to the courthouse. They both knew the odds were stacked against her. It was only Alissa's first time petitioning the state to regain custody of Henry and Faith. Getting them back on the first try was the exception, not the rule. Which Alissa kept reminding herself of, emotionally preparing for what would happen if things didn't go her way.

"Ready, Faith Faith?" Alissa asked while Claire parked.

"Got everything you need?" Claire asked Alissa.

"Yeah, lemme just check my seat again."

"Good idea."

"Okay, let's go."

For all Alissa's anxiety, even having this opportunity to be with Faith wasn't lost on her. Faith had slept over at Alissa's apartment the night before, on a rare overnight pass, and a scarce opportunity for them to be alone together. Henry and Alissa had a married-couple-like relationship. They'd yell at each other, then seconds later would be back to making each other laugh. But Faith was infatuated with her mother. Even when she'd take her to the park, Faith never wanted to play with the other kids or climb on the structures. She only wanted to sit on her mother's lap, taking selfies with her, absorbing as much of Alissa as she could.

A few months prior, Faith had turned four and Alissa threw her daughter a *Trolls*-themed birthday party. Claire pitched in and they rented a private room at a local pizza parlor, transforming it into the *Trolls* fantasyland of Faith's dreams. Adorning everything with the brightly colored animated icons: the tablecloths, paper plates, the cake. Allowing the soundtrack to emanate from the speakers, playing "Can't Stop the Feeling," "Get Back Up Again," and "True Colors" on repeat. The event was a triumph, with Faith spending the day by Alissa's side, taking in the fruits of her mother's labor. But its success, and Faith's elation, could only temper so much of Alissa's guilt. Both about the time she'd already spent away from her kids, and about her lack of control over how much more time she'd be without them.

This guilt never left Alissa for long, and as she walked into the courthouse, she attempted to silence it. Going over what she planned to say to the judge, thinking back on everything she'd learned at Better Together. The coaching she'd received, the months of preparation, all leading to this moment.

"Do you know what floor we're going to?" Claire asked Alissa.

"Here's the room number," Alissa responded.

"Okay. Looks like we're up here."

"Let's go, Faith Faith!"

Outside the judge's chamber was a separate room where Alissa and Claire were instructed to wait. The space was flooded with people: those coming before the judge, and those they'd brought along for emotional support. Mary soon joined them, as did Alissa's social worker. The whole experience felt like being at the DMV. The fluorescent lighting, the well-worn chairs, the too-close proximity of the fellow patrons. A feeling of claustrophobia, permeating the air, keeping everyone in the room anxious and on edge. After sitting there for what felt like an indeterminate amount of time, Alissa's name was finally called.

"I just need to run to the bathroom first," Alissa said when she heard it.

"Don't you think we should head back?" Claire asked.

"I feel really weird all of a sudden. Tell them I'll be right there."

"Mary can go ahead with Faith and let them know. I'll wait for you."

"Thanks, Mom."

Alissa stood in front of the sink, letting the water get warm while she stared at herself in the mirror. Now feeling more physically off than psychologically, she reminded herself that her nerves were likely fucking with her. The magnitude of the meeting was too vast for her mind to comprehend, so her body was processing it instead. Once the water was the appropriate temperature, she splashed a handful onto her face, allowing it to linger there for a second before dabbing the drops off. Only lightly pressing the paper towel to her skin, not wanting to smudge any of the makeup she'd carefully plastered on early in the morning. Hoping to still look perfect in front of the judge.

"How are you doing, honey?" Claire asked, walking into the bathroom.

"Still weird," Alissa said.

"Why don't we go sit for a second before we go in."

"Yeah. Maybe that will help."

In learning how Alissa met her end, all I could think about was that it was the complete inversion of what had happened to Elissa. Elissa's case of encephalitis had come on slowly, without any drastic symptoms or preceding events that would worry friends and family. Its severity sneaking up so fast, so subtly, that by the time they realized what was truly happening, it was too late. While Alissa's sickness seemed to announce itself in a flash, before petering out over time.

She'd made it just a few feet out of the bathroom before she collapsed to the floor. Convulsing on the ground as her social worker cradled her head in his hands, making sure that she didn't swallow her tongue. Claire standing there, trying to organize the chaos around her and remain calm. Going through the motions, making sure to do everything she possibly could to get Alissa to the hospital as fast as possible. Trying not to focus on the total injustice of it all. Which is all I can think about when Claire shares this story with me, the cruel irony.

Alissa's collapse was the first of three grand mal seizures she'd suffer that day, the second coming after the paramedics had already arrived and brought her to a nearby hospital. This one putting her into cardiac arrest, requiring the doctors to perform twelve minutes of CPR before she was revived. Leading them to put her in a medically induced coma.

Alissa spent over two weeks in the hospital fighting septicemia, renal failure, kidney failure. Until the seventeenth day, when her body gave out, surrendering to a mix of these conditions along with a negative medication interaction between the bupropion and methadone she was taking. But the only way I could process what had happened to Alissa's body was the metaphor by which I comprehended how encephalitis had ravaged Elissa's. That same tidal wave breaking free in her body, obliterating all in its wake.

————

Learning the particulars of Alissa's death, my thoughts return to Ponca Pines. I've spent so much time wondering what it was about this school, what could've possibly happened while they were there, that I failed to see the answer right in front of me. What I've determined is that it was the school's original sin, labeling these girls as troubled teens, that sealed their fate. Everything that followed just exacerbated it.

While being a rebellious teenage girl is an inherently romantic experience—one that's been fetishized by the stories I grew up on, both in the tabloids I devoured and in the pages of the novels that I sought refuge in—the romance doesn't last long. There's a very short window between the time in which society places these girls and their exploits on a pedestal and when they decide their escapades have gone too far, are too much. Turning on them for their refusal to conform to the standards of upper-middle-class white morality. Maligning them, sidelining them, and shaming them. Labeling them as bad, or in the cases of Elissa, Alyssa, and Alissa, troubled.

It's a trajectory that I've observed time and time again in Hollywood. Our deification and subsequent dismissal of women like Casey Johnson, Carrie Fisher, Judy Garland. Culture's obsession with the rise and fall of young women being so ubiquitous in the stories I was consuming that I couldn't comprehend the effects this narrative had on the women themselves until I saw them firsthand. Realizing that the societal pressures facing Peaches Geldof or Edie Sedgwick were the same ones that Elissa, Alyssa, and Alissa also grappled with. The labels that had been placed on them and the judgment they'd incurred had isolated them, making them more susceptible to addiction or vice. Leading them to fall prey to the ultimate price of being part of their lineage. That danger I so feared would come for Elissa, coming for them all.

Afterword

The first Al-Anon meeting I ever attended was over Zoom. It was
the height of the pandemic and I'd sublet a room in a duplex just
outside of West Hollywood—with sprawling mahogany floors,
yellow-tiled bathrooms, and a white stucco fireplace—thinking
the gauzy, casual glamour of Southern California would be the
antidote to the malaise I was experiencing. But when I unloaded
on a friend about my mental state—how depleted I was feeling from spending my days talking about so much tragedy and
addiction—her response made me realize that the feelings I was
expressing might be about more than my book. She suggested I
check out an Al-Anon meeting.

Sitting at the oversized dining room table just off the kitchen
of the duplex, I poured myself a glass of sauvignon blanc (something I imagined was an Al-Anon no-no, but still indulged in)
and logged in to my first meeting. Much of the hour failed to reso-
nate with me. Many people talked about their struggles to care for
themselves. These women so unfamiliar with their own needs that
they were unable to recognize them. I'd approached the meeting
with a clear purpose, much like I had all the times I'd gone to

therapy beforehand. Wanting to extract as much advice as possible and apply it directly to my life and the process of writing my book, I was disappointed when I left without action items.

After the meeting, I started looking further into the program. Al-Anon was founded in 1951 by Lois Wilson, who was married to Alcoholics Anonymous co-founder Bill Wilson. Her aim was to support the wives and other family members of those in AA. She found that families of addicts often suffer from a codependence to the drama of their addict's life. It becomes its own form of addiction to distract themselves from their own problems such as the ups and downs and pitfalls of loving an addict. It was a concept that felt familiar to me, though I'd never put those feelings into words. Enough that I vowed to go back.

The similarities I extracted from the meetings themselves were small in the beginning. Most of the time it was the program's catchphrases that spoke to me. Like the idea that you can give the people in your life mulch and water but you can't make them tend their garden. Analogies that I would jot down in my Notes app, returning to them as reminders when I'd inevitably pick a fight with either of my parents. Until one woman shared her childhood fear that her parent would drop off the face of the earth. That they'd go out one day and not come back, never to be heard from or seen ever again. Making me flash back to all those times I'd call my dad while he was off partying with his friends at the country club, his phone ringing and ringing with no reply. The fears I'd harbored about my mother's emotional stamina, after the life she'd envisioned for herself collapsed. That premonition I'd had about Elissa.

I've always felt more comfortable in the chaos of others' lives than the monotony of my own. Involving myself in the financial and social concerns of my parents. Making myself Elissa's emotional outlet. Subconsciously seeking out surrogates for her, friends with their own sets of problems that I tended like a garden that I would weed and supply mulch to. Hoping to heal them to make up for how I felt I'd failed Elissa.

Al-Anon teaches that if we grow used to a certain set of behaviors, we'll stick with them long after they stop serving us. That it's more comfortable to stick with the uncomfortableness we know than that of trying to change. Helping me realize that busying myself with others' problems is what fuels me. Allowing me to be the one who feels helpful, validated, special. The perfect one, even if only by comparison.

It's been a year and a half since I started attending weekly meetings, and I still haven't fully shed these behaviors. At times they're still my coping mechanism, the way I've derived my sense of purpose for so long. But having space to talk about these behaviors—as well as the people who have contributed to them, and the people I've inflicted them upon—has been remarkably freeing. A freedom that I would recommend to anyone who has a loved one whose life has been touched by addiction or tragedy.

Because it was also in this space that I found permission to fully feel my grief and all that it encompasses. No longer carrying it around like some shameful secret, embarrassed by how long I've held on to it. Allowing me to start making peace with my grief. This inextricable part of me, the pieces of myself that Elissa will always help define.

Acknowledgments

Abby, to say this book wouldn't be possible without you doesn't do you justice. From sitting on the living room floor attempting to make sense of what this book could possibly be, to our one million and one notes chats, to all the well-deserved and much-needed glasses of wine on the in-between—thank you for being my rock (and my Raquel). Mollie, thank you for immediately coming on board and for always trusting in my ability to tell this story. Having both your support and unwavering belief in my work has made all the difference. Krishan, thank you for giving me the space and support to tell this story on my terms. You never once shied away from a new idea, a pivot in direction, or another layer. And with this freedom, you allowed me to tell the story of my dreams.

Mom, thank you for being my sounding board, my support system, and my endless cheerleader. You carried the emotional burden of this book for three years without ever complaining or doubting me. Dad, thank you for never once trying to dissuade me from following my dreams. Not for one moment did you try to talk me out of becoming a writer, or make me feel like there was a single goal that was out of my reach, or that you wouldn't have my back throughout. Ari, thank you for always listening even when you secretly wish I'd shut the fuck up. You're my best friend, my biggest supporter, and my number one hypeman. I love you more than words can say.

Thank you to Mimi, Grandma Nore, Tracey, Sloan, Livy, Rachel, Allie, Dhara, Olivia, Norris, Dylan, Garza, Jazzy, Ben Kalin, Isa, Julia, Amina, Tara, Maya, Kat, Emily, Nancy Jo, Kate, Ali, Winnie, and Darcy.

Thank you to all those who have been through the Troubled Teen Industry. Those who shared their stories with me, those who are out there telling their stories on TikTok, and those whose story is just their own. This one is for all of you.

Notes

CHAPTER I

1. Jamilia J. Blake and Rebecca Epstein, "Listening to Black Women and Girls: Lived Experiences of Adultification Bias," Georgetown Law Center on Poverty and Inequality, 2019, https://www.law.georgetown.edu/poverty-inequality-center/wp-content/uploads/sites/14/2019/05/Listening-to-Black-Women-and-Girls.pdf.

CHAPTER II

1. Matt Richtel, "How to Help Teens Struggling with Mental Health," *New York Times*, April 23, 2022, https://www.nytimes.com/explain/2022/04/23/health/teen-mental-health-faq?smid=url-share.
2. Residential Programs: Selected Cases of Death, Abuse, and Deceptive Marketing, Government Accountability Office, 2008.

CHAPTER III

1. Katie A. Ports et al., "Adverse Childhood Experiences and the Presence of Cancer Risk Factors in Adulthood: A Scoping Review of the Literature from 2005 to 2015," *Journal of Pediatric Nursing*, January–February 2019.
2. Laura Brown, "Rachel Zoe: Size 0 to 8," *Harper's Bazaar*, August 11, 2008, https://www.harpersbazaar.com/culture/features/a328/rachel-zoe-interview-0908/.

3. Rasha Ali, "Beyonce Lost 20 Pounds with a Juice Cleanse. Here Are the Pros and Cons of the Crash Detox," *USA Today*, February 15, 2019, https://www.usatoday.com/story/life/2019/02/15/juice-cleanse-pros -cons-juice-detox-beyonce-lemonade-diet-master-cleanse/2811373002/.

CHAPTER IV

1. Anne Jarrell, "The Face of Teenage Sex Grows Younger," *New York Times*, April 2, 2000.
2. Nancy Jo Sales, "Sex and the High School Girl," *New York*, September 29, 1997.
3. Carol Gilligan, "Looking Back to Look Forward: Revisiting in a Different Voice," *Classics@* 9 (Washington, DC: Center for Hellenic Studies, 2011).

CHAPTER VII

1. Rachel Aviv, "The Shadow Penal System for Struggling Kids," *New Yorker*, October 11, 2021.
2. Emily Baumgaertner, "How Many Teenage Girls Deliberately Harm Themselves? Nearly 1 in 4, Survey Finds," *New York Times*, July 2, 2018, https://www.nytimes.com/2018/07/02/health/self-harm-teenagers-cdc .html.
3. Tori DeAngelis, "A New Look at Self-Injury," *Monitor on Psychology*, July/ August 2015.

CHAPTER IX

1. Samantha Bothwell, "Eating Disorders among Adolescents," Eating Disorder Hope, https://www.eatingdisorderhope.com/risk-groups/eating -disorders-adolescents; "Eating Disorder Statistics," South Carolina Department of Mental Health, http://www.state.sc.us/dmh/anorexia /statistics.htm.

2. Jane Morris and Sara Twaddle, "Anorexia Nervosa," *BMJ*, April 2007.

3. Daniel Le Grange, "The Maudsley Family-Based Treatment for Adolescent Anorexia Nervosa," *World Psychiatry*, October 2005.

4. Walter Vandereycken, "Can Eating Disorders Become 'Contagious' in Group Therapy and Specialized Inpatient Care?," *European Eating Disorders Review*, July 2011.

CHAPTER X

1. Tyler Kingkade, "Women Say a School for Troubled Teens Punished Girls for Being Gay," BuzzFeed News, September 8, 2018.

2. Brian D. Earp et al., "Addicted to Love: What Is Love Addiction and When Should It Be Treated?," *Philosophy, Psychiatry & Psychology*, March 2017.

3. M. D. Scofield et al., "The Nucleus Accumbens: Mechanisms of Addiction across Drug Classes Reflect the Importance of Glutamate Homeostasis," *Pharmacological Reviews*, July 2016.

CHAPTER XI

1. David Fuchs, "Utah Has Seen Abuse in 'Troubled Teen' Programs for Decades. Now, Momentum Slowly Builds for Change," *KUER 90.1*, December 17, 2020.

2. Christopher Smith, "Tough Love Proves Too Tough," *High Country News*, June 10, 1996.

CHAPTER XII

1. Valentina Orlando et al., "Gender Differences in Medication Use: A Drug Utilization Study Based on Real World Data," *International Journal of Environmental Research and Public Health*, June 2020.

2. Matt Richtel, "'The Best Tool We Have' for Self-Harming and Suicidal Teens," *New York Times*, August 27, 2022.

CHAPTER XIII

1. Ellen Behrens and Kristin Satterfield, "A Multi-Center Study of Private Residential Treatment Outcomes," *Journal of Therapeutic Schools*, January 2011.

CHAPTER XIV

1. Suniya S. Luthar, Phillip J. Small, and Lucia Ciciolla, "Adolescents from Upper Middle Class Communities: Substance Misuse and Addiction across Early Adulthood," *Development and Psychopathology*, February 2018.

CHAPTER XV

1. Center for Substance Abuse Treatment (US), *Trauma-Informed Care in Behavioral Health Services* (Rockville, MD: Substance Abuse and Mental Health Services Administration, 2014).

CHAPTER XVII

1. Maia Szalavitz, "Opioids Feel Like Love. That's Why They're Deadly in Tough Times," *New York Times*, December 6, 2021.
2. Theodore J. Cicero et al., "The Changing Face of Heroin Use in the United States: A Retrospective Analysis of the Past 50 Years," *JAMA Psychiatry*, July 2014.

CHAPTER XVIII

1. Ulrich W. Preuss et al., "Bipolar Disorder and Comorbid Use of Illicit Substances," *Medicina,* November 2021.

CHAPTER XIX

1. Jill B. Becker, Michele L. McClellan, and Beth Glover Reed, "Sex Differences, Gender and Addiction," *Journal of Neuroscience Research*, July 2017.